The Logic of Education

The Students Library of Education

The Logic of Education

P. H. Hirst

*Professor of Education,
King's College, University of London*

and

R. S. Peters

*Professor of the Philosophy of
Education, University of London
Institute of Education*

London

Routledge & Kegan Paul

First published 1970
by Routledge and Kegan Paul Ltd.
Broadway House,
68-74 Carter Lane,
London EC4V 5EL
Reprinted 1971
Reprinted 1972
Printed in Great Britain by
Redwood Press Limited
Trowbridge, Wiltshire
© P. H. Hirst and S. R. Peters 1970
ISBN 0 7100 6947 2 (c)
ISBN 0 7100 6948 0 (p)

THE STUDENTS LIBRARY OF EDUCATION has been designed to meet the needs of students of Education at Colleges of Education, and at University Institutes and Departments. It will also be valuable for practising teachers and educationists. The series takes full account of the latest developments in teacher-training and of new methods and approaches in education. Separate volumes will provide authoritative and up-to-date accounts of the topics within the major fields of sociology, philosophy and history of education, educational psychology, and method. Care has been taken that specialist topics are treated lucidly and usefully for the non-specialist reader. Altogether, the Students' Library of Education will provide a comprehensive introduction and guide to anyone concerned with the study of education and with educational theory and practice.

J. W. Tibble

The vital contribution which the philosophy of Education, in its modern form of conceptual analysis, can make to the theory and practice of Education, was outlined by Professors R. S. Peters and P. Hirst in their contribution to 'The Study of Education' which introduced The Students Library of Education. This book is a further development and exemplification of their ideas concerning the nature and scope and applications of the subject. The first chapter discusses and demonstrates the techniques used in conceptual analysis. These are then applied in an examination of the key concept 'Education' and of other topics familiar to students of Education – the notion of 'development', the processes of learning and teaching, the limitations and organization of the curriculum, personal relationships in teaching and the nature and purposes of educational institutions.

The book, therefore, as the authors point out in the introduction, serves a double purpose. It presents for consideration a positive thesis about the nature of the educative process, which gives a central position to the development of knowledge and understanding and claims that the emphasis given to public modes of experience, as distinct from school subjects, offers a much needed reconciliation between the traditional authoritarian subject-centred approach and the progressive child-centred approach to Education. It is indeed time that this controversy, at any rate in the crude form in which the recent Block Books have presented it, was laid to rest.

The other main purpose of this book is to exemplify for students of Education in the latter stages of their course as well as for practising teachers, the methods of study which the philosophy of Education in its modern form entails. Readers willing to make the necessary effort will be able to evaluate for themselves the effects on their thinking about Education, possibly also on their practice of Education. For those who wish to pursue the subject at a more advanced level detailed suggestions for further reading are given at the end of the book.

JWT

Contents

Introduction

This book has been produced with two definite purposes in mind. Firstly the book explores the implications for the curriculum, for teaching, and for the authority structure of schools and colleges of an analysis of 'education' in which the development of knowledge and understanding is accorded a central position. It is claimed, however, that within the sphere of knowledge and understanding the emphasis given to public modes of experience, as distinct from school subjects, provides a much needed reconciliation between the subject-centred and child-centred approaches to education. The authors believe that this presentation of a positive thesis about the implications of an analysis of 'education' is more likely to stimulate students to think for themselves about these topics than a more neutral approach to them. They also hope that the point of view which is made explicit in the book will make it of general interest to a wider public.

Secondly the book is meant to serve as an introduction to the growing literature in philosophy of education in Great Britain. This subject has only been recently established in this country and most of the work done is contained in articles and in a few rather advanced books which are suitable only for lecturers and advanced students. This book attempts to explain what philosophy of education is and, by concentrating on its central concepts, to initiate the student into exploring it for himself. It is not, however, designed for students who are just starting their studies in educational theory. Rather it is designed for those who have embarked on the study of philosophy of education as a distinct branch of educational theory. It should therefore be suitable for students in their third year at a College of Education who are beginning serious study in philosophy of education e.g. for the B.Ed. degree, or for students in a Department of Education who are tackling philosophy of education as part of a differentiated education course. With this end in view the authors have included detailed suggestions for further reading for each chapter, rather than studding the text with references and footnotes.

The authors wish to thank *Melbourne Studies in Education* for permission to reprint abbreviated versions of Professor Peters' Fink Lectures on 'Education and Human Development' and 'Teaching and Personal Relationships' which were delivered at the University of Melbourne in July 1969 and published in their 1970 volume. They also wish to thank the Philosophy of Education Society of Great Britain for permission to reprint a very abbreviated version of Professor Peters' paper on 'Education and the Educated Man' which appeared in the 1970 volume of their proceedings.

Finally the authors would like to express their thanks to their secretaries, Mrs Rosemary Snell and Miss Jane Williams, for their patience in typing and re-typing many versions of the text.

I

Philosophy

1 *The contemporary situation*

To be a teacher at the present time should be both disturbing and challenging. There are, of course, many schools where the old routines persist while only the faces change in the classrooms and where, in the staff-room, the conversation revolves only round the idiosyncrasies of the children, the latest idiocies of the government, clothes, cars, gossip and the best places to go for holidays. But more often practices in the classroom are changing as well as the faces and the stock subjects of conversation in the common room are punctuated by controversies about what should be done in the school.

The teacher should find this situation disturbing; for the staff-room may be divided into factions and generate a constant pressure on him to identify himself with one group or the other. Roughly speaking he is likely to find the traditional, more tough-minded point of view and the progressive, more tender-minded point of view. The former will stress the importance of knowledge and skill, traditional subject divisions and the crucial role of examinations; the latter will protest that learning to learn is more important than the actual acquisition of knowledge, that the curriculum should reflect the child's interests and needs, the traditional subject divisions being artificial impediments to the child's natural curiosity, and that examinations are an élitist device whose main function is to encourage a sense of rejection and failure. The former will favour formal class instruction as a teaching method and will not be averse to using punishment to maintain discipline, whereas the latter will favour group projects and individual activity methods and will regard punishment as an unjustifiable expression of the teacher's sadism.

The challenge of such a situation is obvious enough, especially as this opposition between approaches to education represents an artificial polarization, a caricature of the alternatives open to teachers in performing their tasks. There is first of all the intellectual challenge involved in trying to make up one's mind about complex questions to which there are not as yet, and perhaps never can be, definite answers. There is also the practical challenge presented by the real possibility of trying out alternatives to see which is better. There is, of course, the ever present problem of the criteria by reference to which one says that one type of teaching or curriculum is better or worse than another. But at least there exist more possibilities for experiment in the present situation than ever existed before. Indeed, many would say that the illusion is so widespread that change must necessarily be a good thing, that teachers are becoming too easily pressurized into abandoning well-established practices.

It is one thing to find a situation challenging but quite another to have the equipment which is necessary to cope with it. Without such equipment teachers are likely to develop an irrational type of loyalty to one of the factions in the current controversy or to be very much at the mercy of the headmaster or the local 'expert'. It is our conviction that the philosophy of education is an indispensable part of the equipment which the teacher needs in order to form a clearer, better informed and better reasoned opinion about most of the matters under discussion. This presupposes a certain view of philosophy; so something of a preliminary sort must briefly be said about the authors' view of it as an activity.

2   What is philosophy?

Philosophy is an activity which is distinguished by its concern with certain types of second-order questions, with questions of a reflective sort which arise when activities like science, painting pictures, worshipping, and making moral judgments are going concerns. Not all reflective, second-order questions, of course, are philosophical. A teacher, for instance, can reflect about what prompts people to paint pictures or about the connection, if any, between painting pictures and social class. These are reflective questions in that they presuppose that the activity of painting pictures is a going concern. But they are not philosophical questions. Indeed they are part of the domain of two other types of enquiry which are also important contributors to educational theory, namely the sciences of psychology and sociology.

What then, distinguishes philosophy from other forms of reflective enquiry? Let us take an example; for one of the cardinal points in philosophical method is to show points by means of examples. Supposing one teacher says to another: 'You should not punish children by keeping the whole class in' and another says

'That's not really punishing them; and how do you know you shouldn't do this anyway?' The second teacher is dealing philosopically with the moral judgment made by the first teacher. What makes his reply philosophical? What sort of reflection does it exemplify? It involves reflection about the *concept* of 'punishment' and about the sort of *grounds* which are good grounds for making a judgment of this sort. Philosophy, in brief, is concerned with questions about the analysis of concepts and with questions about the grounds of knowledge, belief, actions and activities.

This rather bald assertion should give rise to a host of questions. But two connected questions would obviously present themselves to the practically minded. The first question concerns the nature of conceptual analysis itself. It it, for instance, a matter of defining terms carefully? The second question is how going into the meaning of terms, or probing into the grounds of knowledge, helps anyone to tackle the type of question which sets the enquiry off. Maybe at the finish one's head is a bit clearer than at the start. But whether or not keeping the whole class in is to be called punishing the children, the question still has to be faced whether they ought to be kept in or not. Can philosophizing about the situation shed any light on this very practical problem?

3 Conceptual analysis

Let us first of all address ourselves to the question of what it is to analyse a concept. What is a concept? It obviously is not the same as an image; for, to revert to our previous case, we can have a concept of 'punishment' without necessarily having a picture in our mind of a criminal being hung or a boy being beaten. Is to have a concept then to be able to use the *word* 'punishment' correctly? If we have the concept it might be said, we can relate 'punishment' to other words like 'guilt' and say things like, 'Only the guilty can be punished'. Indeed it was the understanding of this connection that probably led one of the teachers in our imaginary conversation to say that keeping the whole class in did not constitute 'punishment'; for guilt had not been established. This ability to relate words to each other would also go along with the ability to recognize cases to which the word applied.

This looks a much more promising approach to making explicit what it is to have a concept. But it won't quite do for two reasons. In the first place we often make distinctions between things or group things together, but have not got a word for marking the difference or similarity. Are we then to say that in such cases we have no concept? This would mean denying that animals, who make quite complicated discriminations, have any concepts. It would mean that children, who behave differentially towards their mother very early in their lives, have no concept of their mother until they can use the word 'mother'. And what is the point of being so restrictive? Would it not be better to say that our possession of a concept is our ability to make discriminations, and to classify things together if they are similar? To be able to use a word appropriately is a sophisticated and very convenient way of doing this. Indeed it could be regarded as a *sufficient* condition for the possession of a concept though not a *necessary* one. In other words, we would probably be prepared to say that a person had a concept of 'punishment' if he could relate the word 'punishment' correctly to other words such as 'pain' and 'guilt' and apply it correctly to cases of punishment. But the absence of this ability to use the word would not straightaway lead us to say that he had not the concept. He might, for instance, get upset when he saw cases of wanton cruelty but not get upset when he saw cases of punishment; but for some reason or another, he might not have been introduced to the words which have been developed for marking these distinctions.

The second reason why it is not altogether satisfactory to *equate* having a concept with the possession of an ability, whether it be the specific ability to use words appropriately, or the more general one to classify and make discriminations, is that both types of ability seem to presuppose something more fundamental, namely the grasp of a principle which enables us to do these things. Locke said that an idea is 'the object of the understanding when a man thinks' and this is probably as near as we can get to saying what a concept is. But it is singularly unilluminating. As, however, our understanding of what it is to have a concept covers both the experience of grasping a principle *and* the ability to discriminate and use words correctly, which is observable in the case of others as well as ourselves, there is, amongst philosophers generally, a tendency to rely on this publicly observable criterion of having a concept. For it is possible to say more about it than it is about the subjective side. This public criterion is necessary to identify having a concept, but having a concept is not identical with it.

So much, then, for the object of our scrutiny in this branch of philosophical activity. But what do we do in philosophy when we *analyse* a concept? As the concept in question is usually one the possession of which goes with the ability to use words appropriately, what we do is to examine the use of words in order to see what principle or principles govern their use. If we can make these explicit we have uncovered the concept. Historically philosophers such as Socrates attempted to do this by trying out *definitions*. Now there is a strong and a weak sense of 'definition' in such

4

cases. The weak sense is when another word can be found which picks out a characteristic which is a logically necessary condition for the applicability of the original word. Thus, to revert to our case of 'punishment', a logically necessary condition for the use of this word is that something unpleasant should be done to someone. If it were not, if for instance someone who committed a crime were sent on a pleasure cruise, we would refuse to apply the word 'punishment'. Part of our concept of 'punishment', therefore, is that something unpleasant is inflicted. The strong case of definition is when conditions can be produced which are logically both necessary and sufficient. In other words if one can say 'if and *only* if characteristics x, y, z are present, then a person is being punished', we would have a really strong sort of definition. In actual practice, we only have such definitions in artificially constructed symbolic systems, such as geometry, where we lay down tight conditions for the use of words such as 'triangle'. With words that are employed in a much looser way in ordinary language, such as 'courage' and justice', we would be hard put to it ever to find such a tight set of defining characteristics. In conceptual analysis we usually settle for making explicit defining characteristics in the weak sense.

In attempting to make explicit the rules behind our usage of words, and thus get clearer about our concepts, it is important to distinguish *logically* necessary conditions from other sorts of conditions that may be present. To understand this difference is, in fact, to understand the difference between doing philosophy and doing science. It is probably the case, for instance, that acts of punishment are performed only by people with central nervous systems. But we would not have to know about that in order to understand what is meant by 'punishment'. Indeed countless people understand perfectly well what is meant by 'punishment' who have never heard of a central nervous system. The possession of a central nervous system is, therefore, only a general *empirical* condition of punishment rather than part of our understanding of 'punishment'. The connection, therefore, between 'punishment' and the possession of a nervous system is quite different from the relationship between, say, our understanding of 'hearing' and the possession of ears. For the possession of this particular part of the body is inseparable from our understanding of what it is to hear something. We could not conceivably hear without ears of some sort. Similarly, as we shall later point out, it is only an empirical fact that most learning is brought about by some form of teaching. But 'teaching' could not be *conceived of* without some reference to learning. 'Learning' therefore, enters into the analysis of 'teaching' (see Ch. 5); for this connexion is not purely *de facto*.

Now though much of what has been called conceptual analysis seems to consist in looking for logically necessary conditions for the use of a word, and hence to be concerned with 'definition' in a loose sense, it has become fashionable in recent times to deny that it is ever possible to produce such definitions. Ordinary language is not static; it is a form of life. If we think that we have got a concept pinned down, we are apt to come across a case where we would naturally use the word but where the condition which we have made explicit is not established. We might think, for instance, that a necessary condition of using the word 'punishment' is that something unpleasant should be inflicted on the guilty. Yet we do talk of boxers taking a lot of punishment. And of what are they guilty? Wittgenstein made this general point by taking the example of 'games'. He claimed that there is no one characteristic in terms of which roulette, golf, patience, etc., are all called 'games'. Rather they form a 'family' united 'by a complicated network of similarities overlapping and criss-crossing; sometimes overall similarities, sometimes of detail' – rather like the similarities between faces of people belonging to the same family. There is, he argued, no one characteristic or group of characteristics that all games possess in order to be called 'games'.

This, at least, should warn us that we may not always be successful even in our search for logically necessary conditions for the use of a word. But sometimes we may be. Is there, for instance, a use of 'punishment' in which there is *no* suggestion of something unpleasant being inflicted on someone? Actually it can be doubted whether Wittgenstein was even right about this particular concept. For how would we know which samples to lay out in order to look for the similarities? Why did not Wittgenstein take gardening or getting married as examples of games? Does not this show that there is some more general principle which underlies calling things 'games' which he might have overlooked? It might be argued that gardening or getting married might be ranked by someone as games. But this brings out that whether something is a game or not does not depend on any simple observable property of the sort that makes a thing a triangle. Rather it depends on how a human being conceives an activity. A necessary condition of calling something a game is, surely, that it must be an activity which is indulged in non-seriously. Now 'non-seriously' does not mean that the player lacks involvement in it or that he does not give his attention to it. Rather, it means that he can conceive it as not being part of the 'business of living'. He does not do it out of duty or prudence or for any other reason of that sort. This example brings out two points which Wittgenstein himself made. The first is that we must not look for defining characteristics in any simple, stereotyped way, with the paradigm of just one type of word before us. The second is that concepts can only be understood in relation to other concepts. 'Non-serious' has to be understood in relation to a whole family of concepts included under 'serious'.

Thus if we are attempting an analysis of concepts by examining the meaning of words, we usually proceed by taking cases within their denotation and trying out suggestions about defining characteristics. This is how Socrates, for instance, proceeded in the early part of *The Republic* in order to get clearer about 'justice'. He took different cases and tried out suggestions such as 'justice consists in giving every man his due', 'justice is the interest of the stronger' and so on. In this way we gradually make explicit the links between words which reflect our conceptual structure. But we must also pay attention to what we mean by using a word in the sense of the job that we conceive of the word as doing in the context in which we employ it. For words are not just noises or marks on paper; they are more like tools. They do specific jobs in social life. We could, for instance, only understand what 'non-serious' means when applied to games, if we have an understanding of the form of life which renders some things 'serious'.

Obviously one of the main jobs that words do is to convey information, to describe things and situations. But this is only one of their jobs. Sometimes we use words to warn people. At other times we use words to suggest courses of action to people. At other times we use words to express what we wish. And so on. The use of words, in other words, is a form of purposeful behaviour, but it has to be understood in terms of the other non-linguistic purposes that people have in their social life. Commands, for instance, such as 'Halt' have to be understood as having a specific sort of function in social situations where some are in authority over others and where they are expected to direct the behaviour of their subordinates by using words in a certain tone of voice.

Usually the way in which words are put together in what are called 'sentences' gives a very good clue to the job that they do. Sentences can be used to make statements (or assert propositions). When they do this they are usually couched in what grammarians call the indicative form. If we say, for instance, that the motorist was punished for exceeding the speed limit we are stating a proposition that can be either true or false. The job done by the words in this case is, therefore, to describe or indicate a state of affairs that is assumed to have occurred. The point of such an utterance, in other words, is to convey information. But when the headmaster uses the sentence 'Punish the boy' his words which are now arranged in the imperative form, do not state anything that is true or false. They have a different function, that of getting someone to

7

do something. The grammatical form of a sentence can be, however, rather deceptive. When, for instance, it is asserted that a child needs love, it looks as if the sentence is simply stating a fact, or conveying information. But it could be argued that what the sentence is really doing is to lay down standards about how a child should be treated, that it has, in other words, a guiding function. 'Need' in this context, is performing a normative role (see Ch. 3). And there are some words such as 'right' and 'wrong', 'good' and 'bad' which almost always have this general function of laying down standards of conduct.

If, therefore, we are trying to analyse a concept it is important to realize that this cannot be done adequately by just examining the use of words in any self-contained way. We have to study carefully their relation to other words and their use in different types of sentences. An understanding of their use in sentences does not come just by the study of grammar; it is necessary also to understand the different sorts of purposes that lie behind the use of sentences. And this requires reflection on the different purposes, both linguistic and non-linguistic, that human beings share in their social life.

4   The point of conceptual analysis

The question is often put to philosophers when they have done some conceptual analysis: 'Whose concept are you analysing?' The first answer, obviously enough, is *our* concept. For concepts are linked indissolubly with the social life of a group, and it would be impossible for an individual to have a purely private concept of, say, 'punishment'. But, it might be said, there are subtle differences between groups of language users, and though there are obviously common elements in a concept there are also likely to be different emphases and differences in valuation, as, for example, in the case of the concept of 'education' (see Ch. 2). But this type of objection really misses the point of doing conceptual analysis, which is to get clearer about the types of distinction that words have been developed to designate. The point is to see *through* the words, to get a better grasp of the similarities and differences that it is possible to pick out. And these are important in the context of *other* questions which we cannot answer without such preliminary analysis.

Ordinary language is a record of connections and distinctions that men with predominantly practical purposes have found it important to make. It is therefore a valuable guide, but it should never be treated as a repository of unquestionable wisdom. Ordinary usage, for instance, reveals in the case of 'punishment' a connection that practically minded people insist on between the committing of an offence against rules and the infliction of something unpleasant on the offender. In so far, therefore, as we talk about 'punishment' we acquiesce in this demand that ordinary language reflects. Conceptual analysis helps us to pin-point more precisely what is implicit in our moral consciousness. But it also enables us to stand back a bit and reflect on the status of the demand to which the word bears witness. It frees us to ask a fundamental question in ethics which is that of whether this demand is justified. In our view there is little point in doing conceptual analysis unless some further philosophical issue is thereby made more manageable.

The first thing to say, therefore, about the point of doing conceptual analysis is that it is a necessary preliminary to answering some *other* philosophical questions. We cannot tackle the question in ethics of whether there are any good reasons for punishing people until we are clear what we mean by 'punishment'. Questions of analysis in other words are often linked with questions of justification. Socrates raised questions about the meaning of 'justice' because he was also interested in the reasons that there might be for living a just life. But there are also other more all-pervasive conceptual questions with which the analysis of a particular concept is often linked. These are usually called metaphysical questions, those that deal with categories of thinking which structure a conceptual scheme. We employ for instance, concepts such as 'thing-hood', 'causality' and 'time' to make the world intelligible. In metaphysics the status of such categoreal concepts is examined. Could we, for instance, dispense with the concept of 'consciousness' in making human behaviour intelligible? These are general questions about the justification of our conceptual schemes.

The linkage of conceptual analysis with these other types of philosophical question explains the fact that philosophers do not indulge in an undiscriminating analysis of any old concepts. They do not attempt the analysis of concepts such as 'clock' and 'cabbage' unless there are further issues with which the analysis is connected. Questions, for instance, might be raised about clocks if some philosophical issue about the status of temporal distinctions was at stake. There is much about vegetables in Hume's *Dialogues on Natural Religion* because his interest in justification, in this case in the theological argument from design, led him to examine the different types of order in the world. Why should not its order, he asked, be more like that of a vegetable than that of a house? Similarly Aristotle raised questions about the nature of vegetables because he was interested in the general nature of living things and in the role of 'purpose' as a categoreal concept. But without an interest in such further questions what is the point of doing conceptual analysis?

It is difficult to understand, too, how an interest in any such further philosophical questions could itself be self-contained. It is difficult to conceive, for instance, how a person could be interested in philosophical questions such as 'How do we know that we ought to punish people?' unless he is also interested in the moral question of whether or not we ought to punish people. Philosophers often devote themselves to analysing the concepts of the particular sciences and to enquiring into the epistemological status of the methods of enquiry employed. They ask questions, for instance, about the concept of 'the unconscious' and about the validity of psycho-analytic methods in testing hypotheses. But it is often difficult to separate an interest in such general philosophical questions about the status of consciousness from more particular questions about the validity of psycho-analytic theory. Philosophy, as has been explained, is concerned with second-order questions about science, morality, religion and other such human activities. But the point of asking such questions is usually provided by concrete worries at the first-order level. Lavoisier, for instance, was led to make important discoveries in chemistry through an interest in its conceptual scheme. His interests were in part philosophical even though he was professionally a scientist. But he could not have asked such questions in such a precise form without a passionate interest in and detailed knowledge of the phenomena which chemists were trying to explain.

Thus, though a philosopher could be worried about the concept of 'the unconscious' because, like Ryle, he is concerned only with some metaphysical thesis about the status of the mental, he could also be worried by it as a psychologist concerned with giving a theoretical explanation of concrete phenomena. A philosophical psychologist would probably be afflicted by both sorts of worry! A philosopher might be worried, similarly, about 'the state' because he had a general interest of a metaphysical sort in 'the general will'; or he might be worried about it because, like Locke or Burke, he had a practical interest in rights and representation. But in all such cases the concern about concepts has point because of some further concern. To do conceptual analysis, unless something depends on getting clearer about the structure underlying how we speak, may be a fascinating pastime, but it is not philosophy.

Once it is appreciated that conceptual analysis must have some point, it can also be appreciated that the inability to emerge with a neat set of logically necessary conditions for the use of a word like 'knowledge' or 'education' is not necessarily the hall-mark of failure. For, in the process of trying to make explicit the principles which underlie our use of words, we should have become clearer both about how things are and about the sorts of decisions that have to be faced in dealing with them. We are in a better position to look through the words at the problems of explanation, justification or practical action that occasion such a reflective interest. To revert to the example from which we started : that of 'punishment'. An analysis of this concept reveals the connection demanded by men that pain should be inflicted, usually by those in authority, on offenders. This makes explicit much that is of ethical significance. There is first of all a problem about the infliction of pain; for this is usually regarded as something that is prima facie undesirable. How is this to be justified? Supposing it can be, on the grounds that it will deter others from committing similar offences and produce less unhappiness in the long run, than not inflicting it. Why then should it be inflicted on the offenders? For the concept of 'punishment' seems to require this as well. Surely because of some in-built notion of justice that requires discrimination against people only on relevant grounds. But how can justice be justified, in general and in this particular application of the principle? Surely too, the operation of punishment as a deterrent presupposes a very important assumption about human beings, namely that they are responsible for their actions in the sense that they can be deterred by a consideration of foreseen consequences. And is this assumption justified? Is it not an assumption of great moral significance, because of its connection with our notion of man as a chooser? What would happen to our social life if we gave it up? Then there is the connection between 'punishment' and 'authority'; for we can only distinguish punishment from some cases of revenge because those who inflict the pain, like fathers and teachers, are authorized to do this. But what is meant by 'authority'? And can this type of institution be justified? What is the role of authority in social life?

If pursued in this way the analysis of the concept of 'punishment' does at least two very important jobs. Firstly it enables us to see more clearly how a concept is connected not only with other concepts but with a form of social life that rests on a network of interlocking assumptions – e.g. about human responsibility, rights connected with authority, and the role of pain in our lives. We thus begin to get a better understanding of the type of social life to which we seem to be committed if we admit the necessity of punishment. Secondly, however, by laying bare the structure of this concept we also show the extent to which it rests on certain moral assumptions which can be challenged. To discuss their status would take us far into moral philosophy.

Now to what extent would our inability to produce a set of logically necessary conditions for the use of the word 'punishment' be detrimental to these further purposes that lie behind conceptual analysis? Suppose, for instance, we can produce cases of the use of the word 'punishment' where guilt has not been established – as in the case of the schoolmaster who keeps all the class in. Suppose people talk of a boxer receiving 'punishment' when there is neither guilt nor anyone in authority who administers the pain. Surely by reflecting on such cases our understanding of our social life is increased as well as our sensitivity to the complexity of moral issues. We come to distinguish what are often called central cases of the application of 'punishment' from more peripheral ones. The central cases are those in which all the conditions are present which enable us to distinguish 'punishment' from other allied notions such as 'revenge', 'spite' and 'coercion'. The existence of such cases explains how 'punishment' performs a distinctive function in the language which reflects our social life, how people come to acquire the concept, and how people come to use derivative expressions such as boxers taking a lot of punishment. By determining which cases are central we come to learn a lot more, not just about words, but about the structure of our social life and the assumptions which underlie it. If, for instance, we challenge the moral assumptions which underlie punishment we will be led to see what else we may be challenging as well. It is only if we think that there must be some essence in the nature of things or institutions, which our concepts reflect, that we will be dismayed if we fail to produce a hard and fast set of logically necessary conditions for *all* uses of a word. If we do not hold such a crude view of the relationship between words and things we will not measure the success of conceptual analysis by the extent to which we can produce definitions. Rather we will measure it by the extent to which our understanding is thereby increased about how things are in the world and of the possible stances that we can adopt towards our predicament in it.

5 The philosophy of education

It is possible to make a rough and ready distinction between philosophers who are interested in the most general questions about the nature of the world, together with our grounds for knowledge in general, and those who are interested in the concepts, truth-criteria and methodologies of particular forms of thought and activity such as science (including social science and psychology), history, morality, mathematics, art and politics. It is therefore possible, roughly speaking, to distinguish the highly general enquiries of metaphysics, together with logic and theory of knowledge (epistemology) from the more particularized philosophies of a differentiated forms of enquiry, appraisal and action, such as the philosophy of science, history, mathematics and religion, together with ethics, aesthetics and social philosophy. Manifestly the philosophy of education is of the latter type. But it is not a separate branch of philosophy in addition to them; for 'educating' is a very hybrid type of activity. Philosophy of education, therefore, draws on established branches of philosophy and brings together those segments of them that are relevant to the solution of educational problems. There are philosophers of the former sort who sometimes illustrate some general theme by reference to educational concepts. A good example is Gilbert Ryle, who deals with concepts like those of 'training' and 'drill' in the course of defending a general metaphysical thesis about the nature of mind. Generally speaking, however, philosophers of education are specifically interested in educational matters and philosophize in order to get clearer about how things are and about what should be done in this particular realm.

In order, however, to philosophize, the philosopher of education can seldom turn to just one branch of philosophy. If he is interested, for instance, in problems of teaching and learning from a theoretical point of view, because he is simply puzzled about why some children learn and others don't, he will be drawn into philosophical psychology which deals with theories of human development, with types of learning and their relationship to teaching, and with theories of motivation and concept-formation. He may also be led into the philosophy of history, mathematics and science in order to get clearer about what is distinctive of these particular forms of thinking. He is more likely, however, to be practically interested as well, in that he is also actively concerned with questions about what ought to be done in education. In this case he will have also to study ethics and social philosophy in order to arrive at clearer answers to questions about what should be put on the curriculum, about teaching methods, and about how children should be treated.

Assuming that the philosopher of education has both a theoretical and a practical interest in education, it can easily be shown in a more formal way, even at the expense of anticipating the next chapter a bit, what branches of philosophy will be of central interest to him. Educating people suggests developing in states of mind which are valuable and which involve some degree of knowledge and understanding. It is obvious, therefore, that the philosopher of education will have to go into ethics in order to deal with the valuations and into theory of knowledge in order to get clearer about the distinction between concepts such as 'knowledge', 'belief' and 'understanding'. As knowledge is divided up on a curriculum into branches such as science, mathematics and history he will also have to reflect upon what is distinctive of these different branches of knowledge.

Educating people is not done by instant fiat. It takes time, and a variety of different processes of learning and teaching are involved in it. The philosopher of education will therefore have to study philosophical psychology in order to get clearer about the nature of human development and about differences between processes such as instruction, indoctrination, conditioning and learning by experience. Questions about processes, however, are not purely psychological; there are also questions about how much freedom children should be allowed, about whether or not they should be punished, about the authority of the teacher and the rights of students. The philosopher of education will have to go into social philosophy in order to deal adequately with questions of this sort.

In setting out what is central to the philosophy of education in this schematic way we have also set out a structure within which the plan of this book can be located. We propose, first of all, to consider in more detail the concept of 'education', and concepts connected with human development. We shall then discuss what light theory of knowledge can throw on the content of the curriculum. There will then be chapters on teaching and on the personal relationships appropriate to it. The monograph will end with a chapter on the educational community in which the role of authority, discipline and punishment in education are considered against the wider background of the difficulties which educational institutions have to face in carrying out their central purpose.

In a monograph of this sort, which is in part an introduction to the subject, much must be omitted. There is, for instance, no treatment of the fundamental issues of justification which lie behind the view of education developed in this book and behind the assumptions about how children should be treated—i.e. with respect, fairness and regard for their freedom. If then, the conceptual analysis in this monograph is not tailored to the discussion of ethical issues, what further purpose, philosophical, theoretical, or practical determines it?

The purpose underlying the conceptual analysis in this book is really to indicate the implications for teaching, for the curriculum, for relationships with pupils and for an educational community, of taking a certain view of education and of human development. In the context of what the authors regard as the outmoded controversy between the authoritarian and child-centred approach to education a synthesis is attempted which is derivative from an analysis of the concepts of 'education' and of 'human development'. It is argued that if we conceive of 'education' and 'human development' roughly along these lines, then there are important general implications for the curriculum, for teaching, for relationships with pupils and for the organization of the educational community. Of course *detailed* practical decisions in these areas will depend in part on empirical facts which it is the business of psychologists, sociologists and historians to contribute. But such facts are only relevant to practical decisions about educational matters in so far as they are *made* relevant by some general view of what we are about when we are educating people. It is the purpose of this book to show the ways in which a view of education must impose such a structure on our practical decisions.

The thesis of this book, therefore, has relevance at a time when there is much talk of 'integrated studies'. For one of the problems about 'integration' is to understand the way in which 'wholeness' can be imposed on a collection of disparate enquiries. Educational studies are a good example of one way in which 'integration' can be conceived; for studies from psychology, sociology, history etc., can be unified in so far as they can contribute to the endeavour to educate people. The practical purposes embodied in the concept of 'education' provide principles of relevance for drawing on a whole range of enquiries. But these guidelines cannot be provided until we become more explicitly aware of what is involved in educating people. Hence the necessity for an analysis of the concept of 'education'.

It is, of course, open to anyone else to emphasize aspects of 'education' other than those made explicit by the authors. As will be seen in the next chapter, the authors are well aware that their own analysis fastens on certain features of the concept which seem to them to be of particular significance – especially its connection with knowledge and understanding. Alternatively it could be argued that, if this is what is meant by 'education', then perhaps we should not give very high importance to it in schools. For, it might be claimed, too much value can be placed on knowledge and understanding; there are other more valuable things which we might try to promote. To discuss this objection would require an excursion into ethics similar to that required if anyone wished to dispute the demand built into 'punishment' that offenders should have pain inflicted on them. This book, however, contains no such exhaustive treatment of the issues raised by the analysis put forward, though it does contain suggestions for further reading for those who wish to explore them. All it attempts to do is to sketch the ways in which this conception of education must impose its stamp on the curriculum, teaching, relationships with pupils, authority structure of the school or college community. It is hoped that this will do something to deepen our understanding of how we are placed as educators and make more explicit the dimensions in which decisions have to be made.

2

Education

Introduction

Prospective teachers, on applying for entry to the profession, are often asked for the reasons for their choice. Some purely *extrinsic* reasons could be produced which are only contingently associated with teaching. By that is meant that the reasons are not specifically connected with the nature of teaching. They might say, for instance, that they were entering the profession for the money or for the status which it brought. But money and status can be obtained by entering other occupations and the amount of financial reward and status that teachers enjoy varies considerably from country to country. So if that is all that the prospective teacher is after, his or her reasons for choosing teaching as a career would be purely extrinsic to teaching.

A teacher might, on the other hand, say that he (or more probably she) wanted to be with children or that he enjoyed teaching. These types of reasons might be stated more strongly. Doing something for children might be regarded as a vocation; teaching, especially under modern conditions, might be regarded as a very challenging and rewarding way of spending one's time – full of struggles and surprises. Such reasons would be *intrinsic* to teaching, in that they depend upon features of it. But they are rather too general if put forward as reasons for entering the teaching profession. For one could do something for children as a children's nurse or doctor, and one could become a golf professional or driving instructor if one wished only to wrestle with the challenges of teaching. Why enter the teaching profession if one just wants to be with children or to teach?

One way of producing a further specification might be to summon the psychologist. It might be suggested that the individual's choice of this profession might be *explained* in terms of an unconscious desire to dominate for which school life afforded endless opportunities. Or it might be regarded as symptomatic of a refusal to face adult life. Such suggestions might, of course, sometimes have some truth in them. But there are questions about their importance and relevance as a further specification of reasons.

Their importance might be questioned if there exist also conscious reasons which seem adequate to explain the choice. A doctor who decides to operate may be influenced by unconscious sadism. But if there are good reasons, on medical grounds, for his decision, the existence of such an unconscious motive may not be of crucial importance. If, however, the medical reasons are against operating, and if he always prefers the use of the knife to other remedies, the citing of an unconscious motive may be important in explaining his conduct.

If, too, the question is not just one of explaining his conduct but of *justifying* it, the suggestion that he may have an unconscious motive is neither here nor there. It may well be that many who have devoted their lives to medicine, for instance, in the service of lepers, have had also the most surprising unconscious motives underlying their choice. But does that affect its justification? There is surely one type of question about grounds or justification and another type of question about explanation. If people always refrained from doing what there are good reasons for doing because they suspected that they also had unconscious motives which might explain it, then it is questionable whether anything worthwhile would ever be done. For such explanatory questions can always be raised, though they can seldom be conclusively answered. Also that a person sees a good reason of a justificatory sort for doing something is usually regarded, other things being equal, as a satisfactory *explanation* of his doing it. Supplementary explanations, e.g. the appeal to unconscious motives, seem relevant when the reason given is a bad one or when it manifestly does not square with what he actually does.

Are there, then, general justificatory reasons for teaching or being with children which parallel 'medical reasons' in the case of the medical profession? The answer is surely that good reasons for entering the teaching profession derive from the fact that it is concerned with *education*. There also exist educational grounds for doing some things rather than others, when one is teaching, that make one's unconscious motives usually either unimportant or irrelevant. (Supposing, however, that a teacher, without or against educational reasons, always arranges a situation so that he can dominate children, is jealous of others doing the same, etc., or supposing that he always uses corporal punishment, as he says, for the boy's good, when there is absolutely no evidence that it does boys any good, then an examination of his unconscious motives might be both important and relevant.) What then is 'education'? For it has been assumed that there exist reasons deriving from the fact that teachers are usually concerned with education which justify the choice of this profession as well as particular decisions within it. 'Medical reasons' manifestly derive from the promotion of health and the prevention of disease, which are reasons which all would accept. But what, in a similar way, constitute educational reasons?

1 The concept of 'education'

It might be suggested straightaway that there is a close parallel between educational reasons and medical reasons. In the practice of medicine, though stress is now put on prevention, the doctor is mainly concerned with making people better, or curing them. 'Curing' covers a family of processes, such as surgery, the administration of drugs, and so on, whose principle of unity is the contribution to the end of being better in respect of physical or mental health, just as reforming people covers a family of processes which contribute to making them morally better. Similarly, 'educating' people suggests a family of processes whose principle of unity is the development of desirable qualities in them. So 'educational reasons' would be connected with the development of desirable qualities in people.

There are, however, obvious differences, which spring in part from the nature of the ends with which the doctor and the teacher are respectively concerned. 'Curing' someone, on the one hand, suggests that he has lapsed from some standard which the cure is restoring. 'Education', on the other hand, has no such suggestion. It often consists in putting people in the way of values of which they have never dreamt. Secondly there is a general consensus amongst doctors as to what constitutes physical health as an end, though mental health is more indeterminate. About the end of 'desirable qualities', however, there is no such agreement. That is why there is a lot of talk about aims of education; for in formulating aims of education we are attempting to specify more precisely what qualities we think it most desirable to develop (see *infra* pp. 25-8). There is, however, some limitation on what might count as an end in the case of education. For 'education' suggests not only that what develops in someone is valuable but also that it involves the development of knowledge and understanding. Whatever else an educated person is, he is one who has some understanding of something. He is not just a person who has a know-how or knack. There is also the suggestion that this understanding should not be too narrowly specialized.

If this analysis is correct, therefore, teachers who enter the profession because they are concerned about education, would be striving to initiate others into a form of life, which they regard as desirable, in which knowledge and understanding play an important part. The decisions, too, which, as teachers, they take on educational grounds, would be related to the promotion of this general end. Of course there would be great differences amongst them about what constitutes a desirable form of life and some would value some forms of knowledge more than others just as some would place more value on depth of understanding and others on breadth. But at least this general end would give criteria by reference to which decisions taken on educational grounds could be distinguished from decisions taken on personal, economic, or medical grounds. A structure of considerations would also be provided which would render most speculations about unconscious motives unimportant or irrelevant.

The matter however, is not quite as straightforward as this; for 'education' is not quite so straightforward a concept as 'cure' or 'reform'. In particular it is doubtful whether 'education' is always used to designate processes that lead up to a general end in the way in which 'cure' and 'reform' always seem to be used. Doubts can be thrown on this parallel by probing along the lines suggested in Ch. I to see whether any conditions that even begin to look like logically necessary conditions have been provided for the use of the term 'education'. To test this counter-examples have to be produced.

a *Objections to the desirability condition*   Roughly speaking, two types of conditions have been suggested for the use of the term 'education', namely desirability conditions and knowledge conditions. Let us consider first counter-examples to the desirability condition. They are as follows:

i   We often talk of the educational system of a country without commending what others seem concerned to pass on. This objection can be met by citing the parallel of talking about the moral code of another community or of a sub-culture within our own. Once we understand from our own case how terms such as 'educate' and 'moral' function, we can use them in an external descriptive sort of way as do anthropologists, economists, and the like. As observers we appreciate that, in the moral case, their way of life is valuable to them, and, in the case of an educational system, we appreciate that those, whose system it is, consider that they are passing on what they think valuable. But *we*, as observers, do not necessarily commend it when we use the word 'moral' or 'educational' to refer to it.

ii   We can talk of poor education or bad education. This can be met by saying that we are suggesting that the job is being botched or that the values with which it is concerned are not up to much.

iii A much more serious objection, however, is that many regard being educated as a bad state to be in. Their objection is not to a particular system of education, but to *any* sort of education. They appreciate that 'education' has something to do with the transmission of knowledge and understanding. Indeed they probably associate it with books and theories. And this is why they are against it; for they think of it either as useless or as corrupting. Of course they bring up their own children, perhaps in traditional skills and fore-lore. But they do not see any connection between what they think valuable and 'education', and have no specific word to differentiate the handing on of what they think valuable from handing on a lot of other things.

This last point suggests one way in which the objection could be met. It could be argued, with some cogency, that people, who think that being educated is a bad state to be in, lack our concept of being educated. Their understanding has not become differentiated to the extent of needing a special word for referring to the passing on of what they do think is valuable. They have *a* concept of education; for they use the term to refer to what goes on in schools and universities. But they have not *our* concept. The only trouble about this way of dealing with the objection is that people who lack our concept of education are, at the moment, rather numerous. 'We', in this context, are in the main educated people and those who are professionally concerned with education; and 'we' are not in the majority of people who use the word 'education'. So it is doubtful whether the desirability condition of 'education' is a logically necessary condition of the term that is in current use. It stands in this relation to a more specific, differentiated concept that has emerged. This possibility will be considered in more detail later (see pp. 24-5).

Another way, not of really meeting the objection but of accounting for the discrepancies with regard to the desirability condition, is to suggest that the knowledge conditions are the only proper logical conditions, and that the desirability condition is dependent on them. On this view the fundamental notion involved in being educated would be that of having knowledge and understanding. Because knowledge and understanding are valued in our culture, both for their own sake and for what they contribute to technology and to our quality of life generally, being educated has come to be thought of as a highly desirable state to be in – but not by everybody. Whether or not the desirability condition is fulfilled would depend, therefore, upon contingent facts about the attitude of people talking about education to the passing on of knowledge and understanding. The desirability condition, therefore, would not be, properly speaking, a logically necessary condition of the use of the term 'education'. It would rather be a contingent consequence of certain people's valuations.

This way of simplifying the analysis has much to commend it:

i It certainly takes care of those who regard education as a bad thing. As, on this view, the connection between education and something that is valued depends only on the contingent fact that people value knowledge and understanding, it is not surprising that simple people or hard-headed practical men are against it. For it seems to serve no useful function in their lives; indeed it may be seen as an influence that is likely to undermine their way of life. If they see that it may help them to run a farm or to cure a disease they may accord a limited value to it, but only of an instrumental type.

ii There would be no need to make any elaborate philosophical moves to deal with cases where we speak of education and educational systems without approving or disapproving of what goes on. Education would be, as indeed it is sometimes called, the 'knowledge industry'. We could talk of it in the same way as we talk of any other set of practices that we might or might not think important.

iii 'Poor' or 'bad' education would simply mark the efficiency with which knowledge was handed on or the worth of the type of knowledge that was handed on.

This, then, is a most attractive simplification of the analysis. Its main feature, however, is that it puts all the weight of the analysis on the knowledge conditions, and it is questionable whether they are strong enough to support it. They must therefore be tested by counter-examples in the same way as was the desirability condition.

b *Objections to knowledge conditions* The knowledge conditions, it will be remembered, include both depth and breadth of understanding.

i An obvious counter-example would be, therefore, that we often talk of specialized education. This objection could be met by saying that often, when we have multiple conditions, we can withdraw one of them by using a countermanding word. For instance, people talk of knowing things 'intuitively', where 'intuitively' countermands one of the usual conditions of 'knowledge', namely that we have grounds for what we believe. Similarly 'specialized' could be regarded as withdrawing the breadth condition of 'education'.

ii We might talk of Spartan education, or of education in some even more primitive tribe, when we know that they had nothing to pass on except simple skills and folk-lore. This objection could, perhaps, be met by saying either that the term was being extended analogically, as when dogs are spoken of as being 'neurotic', or that the people using the term had not yet developed a differentiated concept of 'education' which takes us back to the type of situation which was encountered about people who think that education is a bad thing. As there are a lot of people who talk in a quite un-abashed way about Spartan education, it is difficult to maintain that the knowledge conditions are logically necessary conditions of the term in general use. This point is strengthened by the third objection.

iii The case of 'Spartan education' is just one of a wider class of cases. A little etymological research reveals the fact that 'education' is, or has been, used without this conceptual connection which is suggested with knowledge. The Latin word 'educere' was usually, though not always, used of *physical* development. In Silver Latin 'educare' was used of the rearing of plants and animals as well as children. In English the word was originally used just to talk in a very general way about the bringing up of children and animals. In the seventeenth century, for instance, harts were said to delight in woods and places of their first education. The word was often used of animals and birds that were trained by human beings such as hounds and falcons. In the nineteenth century it was even used of silkworms! (See O.E.D.) Nowadays we sometimes use it in this general way as when, for instance, we talk about Spartan education or when we use it of our own forms of training that do not have any close connection with knowledge and understanding. In other words the older usage still survives.

Arguments from etymology, of course, establish very little. At best they provide clues which it may be worth-while to follow up. In this case, for instance, it seems that the word originally had a very generalized meaning. With the coming of industrialism, how-ever, and the increasing demand for knowledge and skill consequent on it, 'education' became increasingly associated with 'schooling' and with the sort of training and instruction that went on in special institutions. This large-scale change, culminating in the develop-ment of compulsory schooling for all, may well have brought about such a radical conceptual tightening up that we now only tend to use the word in connection with the development of knowledge and understanding. We distinguish now between 'training' and 'education', whereas previously people did not. We would not now naturally speak of educating animals and we would never speak in this way of plants. But we do speak of training animals and of training roses and other sorts of plants.

These counter-examples to both the desirability condition and the knowledge conditions of 'education' make it very difficult to maintain that an adequate analysis has been given of the concept. It is possible, however, that there is some explanation of these counter-examples. It could be the case, in other words, that the cases that fail to fit the analysis could themselves be linked in some way. If we could get clearer about the principle underlying the counter-examples further light would be shed on the concept of 'education' generally.

c *Education and the educated man* As a matter of fact there is another etymological point that may put us on the track of the explanation of cases that do not fit the original analysis. A little research in the O.E.D. reveals that the notion of 'educated' as characterizing the all-round development of a person morally, intellectually and spiritually only emerged in the nineteenth century. It was also in this century that the distinction between education and training came to be made explicitly. This use was very much connected with instruction by means of which desirable mental qualities were thought to be produced, as well as with the drawing out and development of qualities thought to be potential in a person. The term, however, continued to be used, as it had previously been used, to refer to the rearing and bringing up of children and animals, as well as to the sort of instruction that went on in schools. In other words, though previously to the nineteenth century there had been the ideal of the cultivated person who was the product of elaborate training and instruction, the term 'an educated man' was not the usual one for drawing attention to this ideal. They had the concept but they did not use the word 'educated' quite with these overtones. Education, therefore, was not thought of explicitly as a family of processes which have as their outcome the development of an educated man in the way in which it is now.

Nowadays, especially in educational circles, the concept of an educated man as an ideal has very much taken root. It is natural, therefore, for those working in educational institutions to conceive of what they are doing as being connected with the development of such a person. They have become very sensitive to the difference between working with this ideal in mind and having more limited and specific goals, for which they use the word 'training'. Witness, for instance, the change in nomenclature, following the Robbins Report, from Training Colleges to Colleges of Education. Witness, too, the change from Physical Training to Physical Education. In brief, because of the development of the concept of an 'educated man', the concept of 'education' has become tightened up because of its natural association with the development of such a person. We distinguish between educating people and training them because for us education is no longer compatible with any narrowly conceived enterprise.

Now in the analysis previously given of 'education' as being comparable to 'reform' and 'cure' a connection was assumed between education and the development of an educated man. It was admitted that other people may not have developed this more differentiated type of conceptual structure, but it was maintained that it is important to make these distinctions even if people do not use terms in a specific enough way to mark them out. But it could well be that the older use of 'education' is widespread in which there is no such tight connection between various processes of bringing up and rearing and the development of an educated man. It may well be that many people still use the word 'education' to cover not only any process of instruction, training, etc., that goes on in schools but also less formalized child-rearing practices such as toilet training, getting children to be clean and tidy, and to speak with a nice accent. They may think these achievements desirable, though they have little connection with knowledge and understanding. I do not think, however, that the word is now used, except semi-humorously, to talk about the training of animals, and I have never heard it used to honour the labours of gardeners with their plants. At least the concept has shifted more or less universally in these respects from that of the seventeenth century.

It looks, therefore, as if the concept of 'education' is a very fluid one. At one end of a continuum is the older and undifferentiated concept which refers just to any process of bringing up or rearing in which the connection either with what is desirable or with knowledge is purely contingent. There may be uses which link it just with the development of desirable states without any emphasis on knowledge; there may be uses which pick out the development of knowledge without implying its desirability. The more recent and more specific concept links such processes with the development of states of a person that involve knowledge and understanding in depth and breadth, and also suggests that they are desirable. The analysis of 'education' given at the start of the chapter is of this more differentiated specific concept. It will be with the implications of this more specific concept that we shall be concerned in this book.

2   Aims of education

A teacher who enters the profession because he is keen on education, or who makes decisions about teaching on educational grounds, would manifestly not be relying on the earlier undifferentiated concept; for this could provide no grounds whatever for doing anything in particular. How, then, would reasons, deriving from the later more specific concept of 'education', provide guidance? The general injunction to promote desirable states of a person, that involve depth and breadth of understanding, would indicate only a general direction; it would offer no specific guidance.

More specific guidance would have to be obtained by the teacher getting clearer about his aims in educating people. For the function of the formulation of aims is to specify more precisely what one is trying to achieve, one's target in a metaphorical sense. This attempt to specify precise targets also takes over a further suggestion from the context of shooting and throwing, where the concept of 'aim' has its natural home, namely that the end in view is not altogether easy to achieve. Distance and difficulty seem to be endemic to ends that we would characterize as 'aims'. Aims, however, cannot specify states of affairs that it would be manifestly impracticable to bring about. In this respect they differ from 'ideals'. A person can expatiate on his ideals as a teacher without having to raise awkward questions about practicalities. If, on the other hand, he attempts to formulate his aims, he has to have regard to practicalities. He also has to be more specific than he is licensed to be if he is asked about his ideals. An educational ideal, for instance, might be that every child should learn out of the joy of discovery. A teacher's aim, in the same context, might be a more specific and attainable objective such as that every child in his class should be brought to see some point in learning what had to be learnt.

Formulating aims in education must be distinguished from attempting to answer the general question 'What is *the* aim of education?' This is an unhelpful sort of question to ask in this context because the answer must either be a conceptual truth or a persuasive definition. It would be a conceptual truth if it specified an adequate analysis of the general end brought about by processes of education. In other words, if the foregoing analysis of the specific concept of 'education', as the family of processes leading up to desirable states of mind in people involving depth and breadth of understanding, is more or less adequate, then it would be a conceptual truth that the production of this general end is the aim of education. It would be like saying that the aim of reform is to make men better. And to reiterate this would not provide much guidance for the teacher. Suppose, however, that something more concrete were produced as a specification of this general end. Suppose it were said that *the* aim of education is to produce specialized knowledge. Then a stipulative definition would be produced which would have the function of recommending a specific policy. Instead of coming out into the open and saying 'My aim in educating people is to develop specialists' covert support would be obtained for this policy by trading on the suggestion that pursuing this, and only this end, is consistent with educating people. This, it is true, would help the teacher in giving more specific guidance. But the help would be at the expense of conceptual clarity.

Suppose, then, the teacher attempts to specify *his* aim in educating people or the aims of a particular educational institution. What sort of answer could be given? Roughly speaking any answer which could be a more precise specification of what an educated man is considered to be. Features would be emphasized – e.g. critical thinking, specialized knowledge, autonomy, aesthetic sensitivity – which would be part of the teacher's understanding of what it means to be 'educated'. Content would be given to the general form of 'an educated man' provided by the analysis in terms of desirability and knowledge conditions. Arguments, of course, would have to be produced for emphasizing some desirable qualities rather than others. Indeed this is one important respect in which educating people differs from curing them, to revert to the comparison with medicine. For in education there is as much debate about the ends of education as there is about the methods to be adopted to promote these ends. The same is not true of medicine. There is much more consensus about what constitutes being 'cured' than there is about what constitutes being 'educated'.

It is important to distinguish 'aims of education' in these cases from aims of education when the more general undifferentiated concept of 'education' is being used – e.g. by politicians talking about the educational system. A politician or administrator, in an economic frame of mind, might think of education as the means by which a supply of trained manpower is assured. He might think of education purely in this way and have no regard for the endeavours of educators who might in their turn be impervious to the economist's frame of reference. They might be concerned purely with the development of educated men and women. Of course looking at what goes on in schools and universities from this economic point of view is not *necessarily* antagonistic to being concerned with education in the more specific sense. Indeed a teacher might regard the development of responsible citizens, who have the competence to fulfil some occupational role, as his unifying aim as an educator. For him this civic consciousness might be the hall-mark of an educated person. He might, in his approach, concentrate on getting his pupils technically equipped to do certain jobs, and attempt to make technical skill and knowledge the lynch-pin of a person's depth and breadth of understanding as a citizen.

Similarly a teacher might teach a subject such as science with purely vocational or economic ends in view. He might regard him-self just as equipping people for vocations or as serving a national need for trained manpower, without much thought about the de-velopment of the individuals concerned, as individuals. He might conceive of what he was doing just as contributing to economic growth. But teaching science with these limited ends in view should be distinguished from educating people. Teaching, as has already been pointed out, is not necessarily educative. On the other hand, though not unmindful of the nation's needs, a teacher might also teach science because he regarded this form of understanding as central to his concept of an educated person. Whether a teacher is educating people or just training them depends, mainly, on his intentions, on how he conceives of what he is trying to bring about (see Ch. 5). When these intentions are formulated at a fair level of generality we call them 'aims'.

It is essential for a teacher to try to get a bit clearer about his aims; for unless he does this he will not have criteria by reference to which he can determine satisfactorily the content and methods of his teaching. Suppose, for instance, that he is a teacher of French. Is his aim simply to enable his pupils to rub along all right during holidays in France? Does he hope that they will eventually be able to write French? Does he envisage the learning of the language as the best way of coming to understand, from the inside, the form of life of another nation? Or is his aim just the non-educational one of getting through an examination that will open the door to a range of occupations? Unless he asks himself questions of this sort he will have no clear guide-lines for determining the content and methods of his teaching. 'Education' implies processes of learn-ing; so how can content and method be combined so that learning will result of the type that is aimed at? And how does this contri-bute to the outcome of an educated man? How are processes of education to be conceived?

3 Contrasting approaches to content and method

A teacher could be clear about his aims as an educator, but be wedded to a very crude view about how they are to be attained. For content and methods are not determined *just* by a teacher's aims. He could think of himself as a kind of artist or craftsman using a variety of processes to turn out a desirable product. If he were sophisticated he might argue that 'educate' is derived from the Latin 'educare', which means 'to train', and that his job is to shape the development of children in accordance with a pre-determined pattern. His job is to lick the boys into shape.

This way of conceiving of education draws attention to the inescapably directive function of the teacher, as well as to the desirability condition of 'education'. It makes implicit the fact, which too many gloss over, that a teacher must have views about what are good or bad forms of development and that he is in a position of responsibility in relation to others who have potentialities for both. But it makes this cardinal point in too crude and harsh a way, which does little justice to what is distinctive of educational processes. First of all notions such as 'mould' and 'shape' are being applied in a very figurative way; for the human mind is not composed of stuff or material that can be 'shaped' or 'processed' like clay or wood. If a person is to develop in knowledge and understanding (which is part of our understanding of what being 'educated' involves) he must, in some way, be brought to learn and understand. Maybe extrinsic aids can be used to facilitate this, but *teaching* processes, as will be argued in Ch. 5, are quite unlike any causal transactions with the physical world of the sort that are involved in shaping material. Some kind of *content* has to be displayed, expressed, or marked out so that the learner can master it and make it his own. Methods such as indicating, explaining, questioning and exhibiting, which are employed to transmit such content, bear no resemblance to processes of shaping or moulding. Coming to know something is not at all like having one's hair shaped by a hairdresser.

Secondly the metaphor of 'shaping' carries with it implications about how learners are to be treated to which there are grave moral objections. It suggests that the learner's point of view and dignity as a human being are to be disregarded and that little value is to be placed on his freedom. He is not to be treated as a chooser, as a determiner of his own destiny. An authoritarian method of teaching is suggested to which the most desirable form of response on the part of the learner is the unquestioning acceptance of doctrines.

Progressive education, whose ideals can be found embedded in many sections of the recent Plowden Report, can only be understood as a reaction against such authoritarian conceptions of content and method. Typically the authoritarian teacher thought his job was to equip children with essential skills such as reading, writing, and arithmetic, to fill their heads with necessary information, to discipline them in certain sophisticated intellectual achievements, and mould their characters into a desirable shape. Children were regarded as rather like adults but more wayward, and with original sin rather prominent in their make-up. Methods were used which emphasized formal instruction and learning by heart. Children were instructed *en bloc* without careful attention to individual differences, and this paramilitary operation was usually backed up by the extrinsic aids of punishment and other forms of coercion.

The revolt of the progressives against this system was partly moral and partly psychological. From Rousseau onwards they made a moral protest against the lack of respect shown to children. Children, it was claimed, were not treated at all as moral beings with a right to enjoy their own very different world, but as little manikins who must, from the very first, be forced into an adult strait jacket. Their right to freedom was disregarded; they were victims of cruelty and needless oppression. From the point of view of learning, too, the authoritarian system was unenlightened; for it took no account of recent advances in the understanding of man deriving from Darwin. Children must now be seen as inhabiting a twilight world between man and the animal kingdom. Their minds operate very differently from those of adults and they only gradually emerge, stage by stage, to an adult form of experience. Teaching, therefore, which is not carefully adapted to their stage of development, is bound to be ineffective. Abstract instruction, for instance, is quite inappropriate for beings who can only think in a very concrete way. Darwin, too, had drawn attention to the motivational dimension of experience in his doctrine of instincts. The old system was criticized as being too intellectualistic and too much imposed from without. Children will not learn, it was argued, unless their interests are enlisted and unless learning is self-originated, arising from some instinctual source within them. Finally Darwin's cousin, Francis Galton, had laboriously demonstrated the reality and importance of individual differences, tests for which were not slow to develop once it became widely appreciated that modern industrial society needed a vast supply of relevantly trained manpower.

This combination of moral outrage and biologically based insight led to the advancing of new methods, especially with young children. Importance was attached to taking account of children's stage of development, of waiting till they were 'ready' to learn what had to be learnt from experience. Their interests had to be built upon and they had to become 'the agents of their own learning' instead of always being told things. A more individualized curriculum was advocated which was carefully related to individual differences.

Unfortunately, however, the biological background from which, in part, this revolt derived, became ascendant and the moral aspects of the revolt became overshadowed by it. A generalized view of education, consistent with the assumption that 'education' was derived from the Latin 'educere' meaning 'to lead out', developed.

The aim of education was thought of as 'growth' or the development of individual potentialities; the curriculum, it was argued, should arise from the needs and interests of children, not from the demands of the teacher; methods were only educative if they involved learning from experience rather than being told things and if the child was a discoverer rather than a listener. Doctrines that were eminently defensible as a corrective became erected into a positive panacea.

Criticisms could be mounted against the progressive conception of education in respect of its general woolliness and indeterminacy with regard to aims and content. What, for instance, does 'growth' amount to as an end of education? And does not a curriculum arise as much from the demands of society and the history of man's attempt to understand and appreciate the world as it does from children's needs and interests? But a more fundamental criticism is that this way of conceiving of education represents an escape from moral responsibility under the cover of a biological metaphor. Whether teachers like it or not a teaching situation is a directive one in which decisions about what is desirable are being made all the time. A classroom is a controlled situation and the experience of children is, or should be, structured towards learning some things rather than others. No teacher can stand aside and let a child 'grow' into a Marquis de Sade, any more than he is indifferent whether children learn science, astrology or skittles. The progressives really assumed a traditional curriculum content. What lay behind their emphasis on 'growth' was the moral ideal of 'autonomy' or 'self determination'. This moral ideal was confused with the biological theory, going back to Aristotle, that organic change comes about through the actualization of innate potentialities (see Ch. 3).

It was salutary for progressives to emphasize ideals such as autonomy and critical thought in the context of the authoritarian system; for in this system the teacher had been altogether too directive. Education had been conceived too much in terms of a set stock of information, simple skills, and static conformity to a code. The progressives, in revolt, stressed qualities of mind such as critical thought, creativeness and autonomy. But they did not sufficiently appreciate that these virtues are vacuous unless people are provided with the forms of knowledge and experience (see Ch. 4) to be critical, creative and autonomous *with*. People have to be trained to think critically; it is not some dormant seed that flowers naturally. It is largely a product of the company which people keep, from which they pick up the mode of experience which enables them to manage on their own. Being critical must be distinguished from being merely contra-suggestible, just as being 'creative' must be distinguished from mere self-expression. Both presuppose mastering a mode of experience and being trained in techniques. Both also presuppose a mastery of some body of knowledge. It is pointless being critical without some content to be critical *of*; autonomy, or following rules that one has accepted for oneself, is an unintelligible ideal without the mastery of a body of rules on which choice can be exercised. The romantic protest, in other words, presupposes some kind of a classical background.

The authoritarians emphasized content, but they regarded this as material to be learnt and believed. They valued obedience more than they valued independence of mind. In their system, therefore, there had been little emphasis on initiating people into the mode of experience or way of thinking by means of which it could also be criticized and adapted to new circumstances. Scientific laws and facts were taught rather than the critical attitudes and ways of thinking of a scientist; moral conformity was insisted on, but not moral awareness.

These, then, are two rather extreme polarized conceptions of how content and method can be related for the implementing of education aims. Neither is adequate in itself, though both emphasize points that need emphasis, in too extreme a way. When comparing authoritarian with child-centred approaches to education it is often said that the former were strong on aims and content but weak on methods, whereas the latter are strong on methods but weak on aims and content. There is something in this criticism, but from the authors' point of view they both shared a common weakness – they paid too little attention to *public forms of experience* which, in our view, are absolutely central to the development of knowledge and understanding. And an emphasis on forms of experience can provide a much needed synthesis between these two approaches to education as we shall argue at more length in our next chapter. For content is necessary for modes of experience to be acquired, as well as being important in its own right. And without training in public modes of experience the progressive ideals of autonomy, creativeness, and critical thought are empty uplift.

4 The needs and interests of children

It might be said that scant justice has been done to the child-centred approach to education in respect of the content of education; for nothing has been said about the connection postulated between content and the needs and interests of children. This approach to content sounds morally enlightened because of its emphasis on the individual as distinct from the traditional emphasis on national need and because of its attack on attempts to mould children into a predetermined shape. It also sounds down to earth because of its psychological flavour and its attempt to deal with the all-pervading problem of motivation in education.

A major book could be written solely round the problems raised by this emphasis on needs and interests. Our treatment, however, will be very brief, selective, and tailored to the general theme of this book. We shall try to show that this approach in fact contributes little to determining the content of education, though it may have more relevance to methods. Its psychological trappings too are deceptive; for they conceal valuative assumptions. In so far as it is informative about tackling the problems of class-room motivation in a positive way, it brings us inexorably back to motivational aspects of modes of experience, and so back to the point which we reached at the end of the last section.

a *The concept of 'need'* One of the perennial problems of education is that of the absence of motivation. Teachers often lament the fact that children do not attend, that they do not do their homework, and that they have to be coerced or cajoled into mastering the elements of mathematics, history and spelling. To suggest, therefore, that teaching should be adjusted more to 'the needs of the child' sounds as if a way of remedying this common condition is being opened up which has a solid empirical basis. But an analysis of the concept of 'need' gives little support for such optimism. Indeed, to a large extent, it is a child-centred way of re-stating what should be regarded as aims of education, which leaves the motivational problem untouched. For analysis of the concept of 'need' reveals that it always involves conceptions of value and that not all needs are motivational in character.

If we say that a child needs something – love for instance, or a bath – we are making a diagnostic type of remark about him. We are suggesting (i) that he lacks something – love, a bath (ii) that what he lacks is desirable in some way. It is necessary *for* some desirable condition, the determination of which is a matter of ethical valuation rather than of psychological research. Desirability can derive from different sources. In the case of *biological* needs like those for food or oxygen, it derives from the norm of survival which is, generally speaking, universally accepted as a desirable condition. In the case of universal *psychological* needs, like those for love and security, the norm assumed is that of some minimum level of functioning covered by the concept of 'mental health' (see Ch. 3, Sec. 3 b). There are also *basic* needs, such as for a bed, in which the norm is determined by the way of life of a particular society. Finally there are *functional* needs, such as that of a carpenter for a saw, or of a teacher for access to books, which depend

33

upon the role or purposes of the individual in question. A child's need for a bath has therefore rather a different status from his need for love; for the need for a bath would be an example of a basic need which is dependent upon a particular standard of living, whereas the need for love would be an example of a universal psychological need.

If, then, it is said that the content of education must be based on the needs of the child, to which sort of need is reference being made? Obviously most things that have to be taught in special institutions such as schools are not ways of satisfying the child's biological needs or his psychological needs like those for love and security. For these needs are usually catered for outside the school. In special cases, if children are starved of food or affection at home, the teacher may have to step into the breach. But in doing this he is acting *in loco parentis* rather than teaching. Most of what is taught in school could only in fact be related to the last two types of needs. Autonomy, for instance, could be described as the need to resist influence or coercion. What is lacking in the case of needs such as these is a way of behaving which is approved of in certain societies. For children are not necessarily mentally ill if they lack these dispositions. To talk about a 'hierarchy of needs' at least draws attention to the different status of needs, though insufficient attention is paid to the differences in the norms with which they are connected. The child also needs to learn some elementary mathematics, he needs to learn to read and spell; for unless he masters these skills he will be unable to fulfil his role as a citizen in an industrial society. Needs such as these can manifestly be satisfied at school. But the nearer we come to the class-room the nearer we come to the starting point of this chapter. For how do 'needs of the child' of this sort differ from aims of education? 'Education', in its specific sense, consists in passing on desirable states of mind involving knowledge and skill. These have to be interpreted in terms of aims such as literacy, numeracy, autonomy, co-operation, and so on. So how does the reference to 'needs of the child' help? For the same sorts of thing appear as 'needs of the child', when we enter the class-room, as we already have formulated as being amongst our aims of education.

It might be argued that references to needs is an improvement because it deals with the *motivational* problem in that it emphasizes desirable states of mind, the absence of which are motivating conditions. But this is only true of some needs. In the case of some biological needs, for instance, it is true. If a boy needs oxygen the absence of oxygen will initiate behaviour that tends to bring about the desirable state. It may be true, also, of some psychological needs. If a child lacks love or security he may persist in attempts to attain them. But this is not true of needs which are related only to social norms. If a boy needs a bath he will not invariably make a bee-line for the bathroom; if he needs to be autonomous he will not, as a matter of course, be prompted to give up his dependence on his peers; if he needs to learn mathematics he will not eagerly get down to his sums. Indeed if all such needs were also motivating conditions there would be no problem about motivation in education.

This point can be made in another way by mentioning the difference between 'needs' and 'wants'. If a person wants something in general he knows what he wants and, other things being equal, he will take steps to attain it, though he may not want what is desirable. If, on the other hand, a person needs something, though he lacks what is desirable, he may not know what he lacks and will not necessarily take steps to attain it. In other words wants are always motivational, needs only sometimes. And as the needs with which the teacher is mainly concerned are not always for things that children universally tend to want, reference to them is otiose if the question at issue is the determination of the content of education. They merely conceal important objectives in education under a pseudo-psychological cloak. They represent a way of attempting to psychologize the educational situation which draws attention away from the teacher's moral responsibility for its content. In this respect they fit into the general pattern of the progressive approach to education outlined in our previous section.

But if the concept of 'need' is otiose in the case of the content of education, is it of any more use in the case of methods? The only needs which would be relevant here would be those in which the absence of the desirable state of affairs is also a motivating condition. And certainly teachers could starve children, withdraw love from them, and deprive them of security, and make the restoration of these desirable states dependent upon their learning whatever has to be learnt. But there is manifestly a moral problem about the use of such crude extrinsic aids to learning. There is also a question about the use of extrinsic motivation generally, namely that of latent learning. For what else do children learn if their learning is always geared to such extrinsic conditions? Perhaps they learn also that effort is only desirable when some extrinsic reward results or when some painful condition has to be alleviated. And is this educationally desirable?

Needs may be relevant, however, in another way to teaching, in that the satisfaction of them may be a necessary condition of learning other things. Such needs would not determine specific methods of teaching any more than they would be relevant to the content of what is to be learnt. Rather they would be implicit in the formu-

35

lation of counsels of prudence to teachers in which the importance of prior conditions is emphasized. A biological need, for instance, is implicit in the advice 'It's no good trying to teach children if they are shivering with cold'. Teachers may have to deal with such biological needs before teaching can proceed satisfactorily. Similarly children may have emotional problems deriving from some unsatisfied psychological need for love or for security. These too may have to be worked out before they are ready to learn other things which they need to learn, in another sense of 'need'. Teachers, also, may teach in a way that ignores children's psychological needs. They may create such a feeling of rejection and insecurity in children that they become incapable of learning. Taking account of children's needs in such cases would be a form of advice to teachers about ensuring general conditions which are favourable to learning. It would prescribe no particular content or method.

It might be argued, however, that there are some deep-seated psychological needs, to which attention has been drawn by psychologists in recent times, that are both motivational and extremely relevant to the content and method of learning. These are the needs for stimulation, novelty and environmental mastery which are closely connected with the old so-called 'instincts' of curiosity and constructiveness. Failure to satisfy such needs might be regarded as stunting to a child's development. As, however, such needs provide an intrinsic rather than an extrinsic source of motivation, further mention will be made of them at the end of the next section on 'interests', when intrinsic motivation is considered.

b *The concept of 'interest'* Similar ambiguities surround the concept of 'interest'; for it can be interpreted in both a valuative and a psychological sense. A teacher may be concerned with a child's interests in the way in which a guardian is concerned with those of his ward. He has to protect the child and consider what is good for him. This is a valuative notion. On the other hand he may concern himself with what the child is interested in, with what catches his attention, with his hobbies and pursuits that absorb him. This is a psychological notion.

The teacher is obviously vitally concerned with a child's interests in a valuative sense. He is, to a certain extent, *in loco parentis* and has to watch over the child's welfare. He has also to consider what is *in* the child's interest, what courses of action are likely to maximise the child's opportunities for furthering his interests. The teacher, in this capacity, has to make moral decisions, and courses of action which he insists on as being in the child's interest, may awaken no response in the child. For people do not always want to do what it is in their interest to do. A boy, for instance, may not want to stay on at school though it is manifestly in his interest to do so. So this application of the concept of 'interest' emphasizes the teacher's moral responsibility, but is irrelevant to the motivational problem of education.

The psychological interpretation of 'interest', on the other hand, has motivational relevance, but its relevance to educational decisions is not so straightforward. If a child is interested in something he spontaneously tends to pay attention to it. His interests are those more permanent dispositions to give his mind to things, which are exemplified in his hobbies and in pursuits which absorb him. Obviously if what is of educational importance coincided with interests in this sense the motivational problem would be solved.

But is there such a coincidence? In what sense could education be based on interests in this sense? Could such interests determine the *content* of education? Hardly – for children have many interests that are educationally undesirable – e.g. blowing up frogs with bicycle pumps. Their interests, too, at an early age tend to be sporadic and evanescent. Sustaining interest is perhaps a greater educational problem than appealing to it. One of the most important things a child has to learn when he is young is to complete tasks that he has begun. Unless he learns to do this he may develop a promiscuous attitude towards activities, a tendency to give them up when their initial appeal fades and when difficulties are encountered. He may tend to live only in the present and develop into a person who falls in with the modern cult of instancy. There is also the empirical point that most of children's interests are socially acquired. They get them from their parents, from other children, and from the mass media. If the teacher does nothing to encourage interest in what is worthwhile he is simply opting out of his responsibility and abandoning children to get their interests from other sources which may be antipathetic to education.

Of course what a child is interested in may also be of educational value. To develop depth and breadth of understanding in relation to this would be an obvious way into a curriculum; for a child might pass smoothly and eagerly along this path into other realms that have to be explored. But there may be many things which he 'needs' to learn in which he has not the slightest interest. So the curriculum itself, as distinct from the point of entry to the curriculum, could not be determined purely by his interests.

This regard for children's interests in teaching has more relevance to the *method* of teaching than to its content. For one of the hall-marks of teaching people, as distinct from just lecturing at them, is that the teacher should start from where the learner is and attempt to lead him on from this point. This is one of the most important aspects of the emphasis on developmental stages which we shall be considering in our next chapter. The same is true in the motivational sphere. Children's existing interests can be used as a starting point from which they can be led on to take an interest in realms of whose existence they never dreamt. This can be done in two ways. Firstly development can proceed in accordance with Gordon Allport's principle of 'functional autonomy' which suggests that means can become ends. Children may be persuaded to study maths or to learn to read because they see these activities as necessary to something in which they are interested – e.g. going shopping, appreciating advertisements. After a period of practice, however, they may come to enjoy maths and reading for their own sake and engage in them without any extrinsic incentive. Secondly they may find themselves becoming interested in things which are associated with the things which they enjoy doing. Indeed their ends may gradually come to occupy the status of means for them. For instance, they may enjoy riding a bicycle. This may take them into the country which is quite unfamiliar to them. But new interests may open up as a result and bicycling may become just a means to pursuing them. Indeed they may eventually pursue them without bothering about the bicycle.

In both such cases existing interests, which may or may not be in things which are themselves of educational importance, have been assumed to lead on to an interest in something which is educationally important. But this raises the crucial motivational question of what it is about educationally important activities which is motivationally potent. What features of them lead children to get interested in them for their own sake? What is it about cooking or doing mathematics, about writing or listening to poetry which is capable of attracting and absorbing children? If more was known about this a more direct approach might be made to getting children interested in them. The route to them via their existing interests might not have to be so often used.

In the psychology of motivation the old classical theories of need-reduction are more or less outmoded in so far as they claimed to provide over-all theories of human motivation. It is now accepted that not all things are learnt because they are related to biological needs. At the human level 'intrinsic motivation' is important. Human beings are curious, enjoy mastering things and constructing things, and have a need for achievement. Learning, it has been argued, has its own motivation in that finding out things, solving problems, and getting rid of incoherences are absorbing in themselves. No extrinsic source of motivation is necessary to account for such activities. But if this form of motivation is going to be appealed to with children, much more needs to be known in detail about the features of what has to be learnt, which are attractive in this way to children at particular stages of their development. If more were known about this aspect of intrinsic motivation teachers might not have to work in such a trial and error way at trying to get children interested in what it is in their interest to learn.

From the point of view put forward in this book the emphasis in such modern theories of motivation on cognitive features of motivation is significant, whether they stress cognitive conflict, dissonance, or stimulation. For our argument when, in Ch. 3 and 4, we go into more detail about what we have called 'modes of experience', will be that 'cognition' is differentiated into distinct modes. It is therefore important to distinguish types of dissonance or stimulation that are specific to, say, scientific, as distinct from moral or aesthetic understanding. Further knowledge of motivating features, therefore, will depend, at least in part, on careful analysis of the content of what has to be mastered in these different modes of experience. There is also the problem of how the interest of children is awakened and stimulated in the appraisals and achievements that are characteristic of the different modes of experience. How, for instance, in the case of science do children come to care about getting their facts right, being clear and precise? How do they come to abhor what is irrelevant, inconsistent and false? How, in the moral sphere, does the sense of justice develop? How does sporadic sympathy develop into respect for persons and animal caution into a more reflective prudence? Little is known about the development of such 'rational passions' which are crucial to the functioning of the various modes of experience. When, in this book, we stress the importance of the development of knowledge and understanding as being central to education, we are acutely aware that the cognitive and affective aspects of such development are intimately connected. Our sympathies are with the progressives in their emphasis on motivational factors in education, to which they drew attention with their talk about the needs and interests of children. But our conviction is that this kind of motivation, which is crucial in education, is unintelligible without careful attention to its cognitive core. The same type of conclusion will be reached when, in our next chapter, we tackle the progressive emphasis on development.

5 The ethical basis of education

It was stressed in the first chapter that conceptual analysis, in a sense, leaves everything as it is. In other words getting clearer about a concept such as 'needs' or 'education' does not, of itself, provide reasons of a conclusive kind for doing one thing rather than another. But, if the concept is worth analysing, in getting clearer about it we should also be getting clearer about the issues of explanation or justification that have to be faced.

Our analysis of the concept of 'need' has illustrated this point very well. It has been shown to be an inescapably valuative concept which is ambiguous; for it indicates the absence of a desirable condition, but its desirability can be judged by different types of criteria. Is the standard that of survival, of mental health, or of approval in a particular society? Analysis helps to make explicit the value-judgments that lie behind statements of need, but, of itself, does nothing to justify them. In this respect it serves just as a prolegomenon to moral philosophy.

We also maintained that, in so far as statements about the needs of children are relevant for determining the content of education, they are merely a child-centred way of making judgments about educational aims. So we are thrown back to problems of analysis which concerned us at the beginning of this chapter about what is meant by 'education' and how 'aims' are related to it. But here again analysis simply sets up further problems. We suggested, in our analysis, that in so far as we are concerned about education in what we called its specific sense, we are committed to processes which assist the development of desirable states in a person involving knowledge and understanding. But how do we determine which states are desirable? And why should knowledge and understanding be so favoured as a necessary feature of them? Autonomy was mentioned both as an aim implicit in the progressive approach to education and as one of the needs of the child that the school should meet. But on what grounds is autonomy singled out as a desirable state? Why, similarly, should we put science and poetry on the curriculum and not astrology and shove-halfpenny? It is no good saying that we do this because we are concerned about educating people; for what is at stake is the justification of education. Conceptual analysis has enabled us to get clearer about what is implicit in this commitment to education. But it cannot, of itself, provide answers to the ethical issues which it helps to make explicit.

Education, however, not only involves content and aims, both of which give rise to further ethical questions; it also involves methods and procedures in which are embedded various principles governing our treatment of children. In dealing, for instance, with the type of extrinsic motivation involved in gearing what has to be learnt to children's needs we queried the moral desirability of treating children in this way. As democrats we probably think that principles such as fairness, freedom and respect for persons should structure our relationships with children. We are averse to indoctrination and conditioning as techniques. We also think, probably, that such principles are important not just as structuring our dealings with children, but also as part of the content of their moral education that they will come to understand and to make their own. But, under whatever aspect these principles are viewed, the question of their justification remains. How is a person, who believes in fairness, to answer someone who is a determined advocate of some form of discrimination? What arguments can the lover of liberty advance against the kindly despot who puts more emphasis on the virtues of conformity and obedience? Or is it the case that different people are brought up in different forms of life, each with their own distinctive moral traditions, and that there are no grounds for saying that one form of life is better than any other?

Any teacher who wishes to work out more clearly where he stands on educational issues must pursue these questions further in moral and social philosophy. If the analysis of 'education' and of other concepts presented in this chapter has done something to indicate a bit more precisely the sorts of moral questions that require an answer, its authors will have attained one of their main objectives. They are conscious that a definite moral point of view is implicit in their approach, but it is not part of the intention of this book to attempt any explicit justification of it.

There are, however, many other questions which still remain even if the importance accorded to knowledge and understanding, built into the specific concept of 'education', can be justified as well as democratic principles such as freedom, fairness, and respect for persons, which are assumed to be defensible in dealing with children. It is hoped that further conceptual analysis of concepts such as 'development', 'teaching', 'personal relationships', 'authority', and 'discipline', when combined with that already undertaken, will do something to elucidate educational issues about which any teacher has to make up his own mind. The analysis already given of what makes them 'educational' should serve to sharpen up features revealed by further analysis.

3
Development

Introduction

It was stressed in the last chapter that progressive education was a most salutary reaction against the traditional system in that it drew attention to the importance of relating learning to the child's stage of development and to his interests. It was also pointed out that its biological approach obscured the inescapably valuative character of education and the directive function of the teacher. These latter features of education were stressed by traditional teachers in too authoritarian a way. However a synthesis was suggested out of the thesis of the authoritarian and the antithesis of the child-centred conceptions of education, by making explicit the role of public modes of experience.

These contrasting ways of approaching education still survive in schools and colleges of education. The subject specialist in a school or college of education might well view his task in terms of the development of specialist knowledge. Other teachers, especially primary teachers and lecturers in education departments in colleges of education, would probably argue that what is important is the development of the child as a person. They might also maintain that a subject-centred type of approach to education is both artificial and a hindrance to personal development. Education, it might be argued, should be based on the development of the child. What has to be shown in more detail, if the synthesis of the previous chapter is to be sustained, is that the notion of public modes of experience can reconcile these two approaches in a way that does justice to the valuative aspects of education and which puts the contrasting emphasis on specialist knowledge and personal development into a proper perspective. In this chapter, therefore, the concept of 'development' will be critically and constructively examined with these ends in view.

1   The concept of 'development'

'Development' suggests changes of an irreversible nature through time, the direction of which is characteristic of that which develops. Ernest Nagel in his contribution to the book edited by D. B. Harris (see 'Further Reading'), gives tighter criteria for 'development' which are taken from a range of cases in which the potential becomes actual – e.g. cases such as the development of a photograph or oak tree. He therefore suggests the criteria of (a) some pre-existing structure, (b) processes which either 'unfold' or are more actively assisted by outside agencies and which are irreversible, (c) some end-state which is the culmination of the process. In biology, due to the influence of the theory of evolution, this end-state was thought of as involving an increased capacity for self-maintenance, and as characterized by an increased complexity and differentiation of functions which are integrated at a higher level of functioning.

There is little difficulty in using these tight criteria when applying the concept to human beings at the physical level. The bodies of men, together with their basic biological functions, develop in this way. The question is, however, whether this concept can be applied with these criteria at the mental level. Let us, therefore, consider each of these criteria in turn, not because they can be applied to mental development in any precise way, but because by seeing where they do and do not fit, we may in the process become clearer about the main contours of 'human development'.

a *Pre-existing structure*   'Structure' implies relationships between parts or items. The most obvious cases of this are spatial relations as in the structure of a house. In the case of mental structure, however, the items are not physical and the relationships are not spatial. This does not mean, however, that the notion of 'structure' has no application; for we can talk of logical structure in cases where some kind of logical relationship holds between concepts or propositions. It is this kind of 'structure' that would be appropriate in the case of 'mental structure'.

'Mental' is presumably to be understood in terms of modes of consciousness such as understanding, wanting, being affected. To talk of mental structure is to suggest that the content of these different modes of consciousness has some kind of logical or conceptual network of relationships. This seems obviously to be the case. In understanding things, for instance, there are rules for classifying them as things of various sorts – e.g. rules for the use of a term such as 'punishment' which relates it to other terms such as 'pain' (see Ch. 1, Sec. 3), and rules for interpreting change – e.g.

43

the causal principle in the case of changes of material things such as soap or ice. In wanting things we impose a means-end structure on experience. Modes of consciousness are also conceptually related to each other. If a man wants something – e.g. another job – he wants it under some description that involves his beliefs about it – for instance, that the work will be more interesting, or that he will have more congenial colleagues.

The case for there being at the human level some kind of mental structure, which is subject to change is, therefore, straightforward. But whether there is much in the way of *pre-existing* mental structure is quite another matter. To discuss that possibility would take us into the heart of the controversy about innate ideas that has ranged from the time of Plato through Descartes, Locke, Leibnitz and Kant, up to the recent speculations on the subject by Chomsky. But there is really no need to go into this if we wish to talk with good conscience about mental development; for the insistence that structure should be pre-existing is plausible only in certain favoured cases, mainly in botany and biology. It is perfectly true that the child development movement in educational theory tried to assimilate the development of a human being to that of a plant with the metaphor of the kindergarten. But few would now support this maturational or unfolding type of theory, and it would seem rather arbitrary to insist that, unless the first condition of pre-existing structure is satisfied, the concept of 'development' is not applicable to the human case.

b *Sequential processes*   Nagel's second criterion of sequential processes of an irreversible sort, on the other hand, seems much more central to the concept of 'development'. How are such sequences of changes in structure to be understood if we are talking about mental development? They are, first of all, manifestly different from those involved at the level of physical growth. An acorn, on its way to becoming an oak tree, goes through various changes in physical shape and structure, with accompanying modes of functioning, which can be observed to occur in sequences. The changes occur because of the physical and chemical reactions between the organism and its environment. Social influences do little to shape its growth. Acorns do not respond to commands, instructions, explanations, and the like. At the human level, on the other hand, stages of development are to be characterized not in terms of physical shape and structure but in terms of the level of understanding, wanting, etc., which has been reached, and the ways in which an individual passes through stages has to be described in terms of his learning. Changes from one level of mental structure to another cannot be described in mechanical terms at all and even the biological model, used by Piaget, of assimilation and accommodation, can only be used metaphorically. For when a child takes in a novel happening by 'assimilating' it to his existing conceptual structure he does not literally assimilate it in the way in which an organism assimilates food. And the process of accommodating, of changing his concepts because the novel happening is too discrepant with his existing structure, is not literally the same as that of accommodation at the biological level.

Furthermore, although the physical environment of a plant influences its development, it is in no sense constitutive of it. The plant does not become like the soil or the sun when it takes it into its system. In the mental case, on the other hand, much of the *content* of development is provided by the social environment. Children model themselves on others. Also, what we call teaching processes have in common the fact that some sort of content – a belief, a rule, a way of behaving – is displayed, indicated, or marked out in some way or other for the learner to make his own (see Ch. 5). The phrase 'make his own' is also significant in the human case. For human beings develop in part because of their decisions and choices. They make themselves to a certain extent. This way of talking is quite inappropriate at the plant or animal level.

c *The end-state*   What, too, at the human level, corresponds to the mature oak-tree or elephant which represents the end-state of plant or animal development? Does not human life offer a great variety of possibilities of development? And do not these depend partly on cultural pressures and partly on individual choice – factors which do not apply at the plant or animal level? And is not our conception of such an end-state irredeemably valuative in nature? In developmental theories either these value judgments have been overt, as in the case of Arnold Gesell, who explicitly took as his paradigm of human development an ideal based on a small sample of what he considered to be outstanding American democratic citizens. Or the ideal can be implicit, as in the case of Freud who, as Philip Rieff has shown (in Rieff, P. *Freud, the Mind of the Moralist*, Viking Press, 1959), presupposed an ideal of man as a cautious egoist, a prudent devotee of the nicely calculated more or less in the realm of satisfactions.

But could there be any conception of the end-state of human development which escaped being tied to the values of a particular culture, and hence being not properly an end-state of *human* development? This question cannot be answered until a more satisfactory account of human development is sketched which lifts the discussion out of the biological realm. In spite of its many inadequacies the cognitive stage theory of Piaget and Kohlberg presents the most illuminating alternative. So this will be used as a method of approach to the problems posed at the beginning of the chapter.

2 The cognitive stage theory

Kohlberg (for references, see 'Further Reading') claims that there are invariant sequences in development which seem to hold in any culture. He produces evidence, for instance, to show that in any culture children begin by being unable to distinguish dreams from real events. They then grasp that dreams are not real, then that they cannot be seen by others and take place inside the dreamer, then that they are immaterial events produced by the dreamer, like thoughts. He makes two points about this sequence which, he claims, hold for all proper developmental sequences. Firstly he claims that this sequence cannot be fully explained in terms of the teaching of adults; for if adults taught anything about dreams they would tend to use concepts about them appropriate to a much later stage, which would not explain how children go through the earlier stages. Also the same sequence can be observed in cultures where adults have different beliefs about dreams. Secondly Kohlberg argues that the stages of development in relation to dreams could not have a different order. It depends upon the relationship to each other of concepts such as 'unreal', 'internal', 'immaterial', which it would take too long to explicate.

a *Invariant sequences in forms of thought* . Piaget has, of course, extensively illustrated this thesis about invariant order depending upon relationships between concepts in the case of maths and elementary physics, and, to a more limited extent, in the moral sphere. Kohlberg himself has elaborated this thesis in the field of morals. He holds that, though there is a difference between cultures in the *content* of moral beliefs, the development of their *form* is a cultural invariant. In other words, though there is a variation between cultures about whether or not people should e.g. be thrifty or have sexual relationships outside marriage, there are cross-cultural uniformities relating to how any such rules are conceived e.g. as ways of avoiding punishment, as laid down by authority, and so on. Children, Kohlberg claims, start by seeing rules as dependent upon power and external compulsion; they then see them as instrumental to rewards and to the satisfaction of their needs; then as ways of obtaining social approval and esteem; then as upholding some ideal order and finally as articulations of social principles necessary for living together with others. Varying contents given to rules are fitted into invariant forms of conceiving of rules. Of course in many cultures there is no progression through to the final stages, the rate of development will be different in different cultures, and in the same culture there are great individual differences. All this can be granted and explained. But his main point is that this sequence in levels of conceiving of rules is constitutive of moral development and that it is a cultural invariant. Also, because of the conceptual relations involved, which are connected with stages of role-taking, it could not occur in any other order.

How, then, does Kohlberg think that this type of development occurs if it is not the result of teaching? He rejects maturation theories as non-starters except in the case of abilities such as walking. He produces evidence to refute various types of socialization hypothesis. He also rejects Kant's view that these forms of conceiving of rules are innate moulds into which specific experiences are fitted. Like Piaget he argues that they develop as a result of interaction between the child and his physical and social environment. Development is characterized by the individual's restructuring of his way of conceiving of the content supplied by his perception of his physical and social environment. These changes in cognitive structure are assisted by stimulation from other people as well as by contract with the objects perceived. But they cannot be brought about by direct instruction.

This interactionist theory of development is applied to the moral sphere. Kohlberg thinks that the stages of development here represent culturally invariant sequences in the child's conception of himself, of others and of the rules which structure his social life. Social and moral understanding develop *pari passu* with other forms of cognitive development. Just as contact with the physical environment gradually stimulates a child to structure it in terms of objects having causal relations with other objects in space and time, to make the distinction between what is real and what is apparent, and gradually to grasp more abstract ways of introducing order into the world, so also in the social and moral case, the child is gradually led to connect social rules with principles, especially that of justice, which must obtain if individuals are to live together and to satisfy their claims as social beings, who are both similar to and different from others. The stages in development are marked by changes in the *forms* of thought about rules defining social relationships rather than by any great changes in content.

Kohlberg's theory of the factors which influence moral development illustrates an important point about teaching which might do much to reconcile the instruction and discovery based approaches to it (see Chapter 2, Sec. 3). He claims that mental development is neither a matter of unfolding what is within nor of stamping in something from without. It is rather a matter of the interaction of a mind, which is to be characterized in terms of its capacity for classifying and discriminating the environment, and the situation in which human beings are placed. Much of the *content* of experience is, of course, culture-bound and passed on by example and instruction. But its form, by reference to which stages of development are characterized, cannot be externally imposed. It is something that the individual has to develop for himself with appropriate 'stimulation' from others and from typical concrete situations. Kohlberg views this finding as providing a psychological rationale for Socrates' conception of education in which the learner is gradually brought to see things for himself – not haphazardly, but in a tightly structured situation. But more would have to be said both about 'teaching' and about 'cognitive stimulation' before this implied contrast between 'teaching' and 'stimulation' could be accepted.

We have dwelt on this particular case of moral development for two reasons. Firstly it illustrates very well a way in which mental development can be conceived. It is not a matter of how much is known or of individual idiosyncrasies of self-expression; it is rather a matter of progression along a public mode of experience whose stages can be charted by reference to the form of experience as distinct from its particular content. The order of stages could not be otherwise than they are for logical reasons in that the later presupposes the earlier and is related hierarchically to it. For instance, one could not, for logical reasons. conceive of the hypothetico-deductive stage of scientific thought preceding the more mundane classifying of the stage of concrete operations in Piaget's account of scientific development; one could not conceive of his autonomous stage of morality preceding his transcendental stage.

Secondly we have illustrated this conception of sequential processes by reference to the moral mode of development rather than by reference to more obvious ones, such as the mathematical and scientific, for the very reason that these features of development might be thought to be confined to these 'intellectual' areas. But they are not so confined. The moral can be charted as a universal form of human development just as can the scientific and the mathematical. Other such modes of experience would have to be distinguished by reference to distinctive structures of organizing concepts which make distinct forms of experience possible (see Ch. 4, Sec. 1b). On this view of 'development', then, a central place is assigned to those same public modes of experience which were picked out at the end of Ch. 2 as providing a necessary synthesis between the authoritarian and child-centred approaches to education.

It might be thought, however, that emphasis on cognitive factors such as distinctive concepts, presents an over-intellectualistic account of development. What about emotional development? Has not this been ignored? And is not this way of conceptualizing human development at variance with that which is most common amongst adherents of the developmental approach to education? This type of criticism is important and based largely on misunderstandings both about modes of experience and the nature of the human mind. So it must be briefly answered.

b *Current classifications of development*   In most of the standard works on child development, studies are classified under the heading of physical, intellectual, social and emotional development. The developing child is thought of as four-sided, though there has been a recent tendency to separate moral development out from the wider realm of social development and thus to construct a fifth dimension. But is this a theoretically valid or fruitful way of conceptualizing forms of development? Physical development can be left on one side, not because it is unimportant but because it does not give rise to conceptual difficulties. But what distinguishes, say, emotional development from social development? And how is intellectual development to be distinguished from either of them? The suggestion seems to be that men have an intellect which is somehow divorced from feeling, and that neither the intellect nor the emotions are social. These assumptions are quite indefensible.

Let us consider emotional development first. Paradoxically perhaps, the central feature of states of mind which we call 'emotions', such as fear, jealousy, remorse, etc., is a type of cognition that can be called an appraisal. A situation is seen under an aspect which is pleasing or displeasing, beneficial or harmful. To feel fear, for instance, is to see a situation as dangerous; to feel pride is to see with pleasure something as ours or as something that we have had a hand in bringing about. Envy is connected with seeing someone else as possessing what we want, jealousy with seeing someone as possessing something or someone to which or whom we think we have a right. And so on. The appraisal in each case has a feeling side to it. If fear is felt, seeing something as dangerous is different, from seeing it as three feet high or as green, in that it is non-neutral. Green or something's height may, of course, in certain contexts contingently affect us powerfully; but it is not part of our understanding of these features of the environment that they should matter to us in this way. With features picked out by states of mind which we call emotions, on the other hand, the connection with feeling is a conceptual one. That is why the cognitive core of the emotion is referred to as an appraisal and not just as a judgment. But the feeling is inseparable from the cognition; we could not identify such feelings without reference to the understanding of the situations which evokes them. Most of such situations are social. Hence the absurdity, also, of separating emotional from social development. Emotions such as jealousy, guilt, pity, and envy cannot be characterized without reference to moral and social concepts such as rules, ownership, and rights. One of the main features of emotional development is the learning of the countless different ways of appraising other people and ourselves in terms of a conceptual scheme which is basically social in character. The education of the emotions consists largely in the development of appraisals of this sort which are appropriate in terms of moral and aesthetic criteria and which are founded on realistic beliefs about how we are placed.

The tendency to disregard the importance of cognition in this area has led to the neglect of the specific features of interpersonal understanding as a mode of experience which is of manifest importance in the recognition of emotions and motives in oneself and others. This is usually regarded as rather a murky field about which little that is clear and precise can be said. It has thus largely been occupied by those who talk in a mystical way about 'I' and 'Thou', and by the devotees of the various brands of psycho-analysis. The result is that the development of stages in interpersonal understanding remains uncharted in any precise way; so also does the development of emotions and motives. Very little has been done in the area of beliefs and conceptual prerequisites. What is presupposed, for instance, before people can act out of remorse or out of respect? What other beliefs and concepts does a person have before these ways of regarding other people and himself are possible for him? What are the connections between the various emotions and stages in the development of moral and interpersonal modes of experience? This specific mode of development should be studied in the same sort of way as the scientific, mathematical and moral modes have been by Piaget and others.

The separation of intellectual from affective development is as untenable as the study of emotional development without stress on the role of cognition. It perpetuates the fairy story that there is a particular part of the mind, namely the intellect, that can be sharpened up and trained by exercise. In practice in the textbooks 'intellectual development' usually amounts to development in maths and science, and of a rather dubious ability referred to as 'problem-solving'. It is understandable, however, why 'intellectual' should be thought of in such a narrow way; for 'intellectual' is more properly related to a disposition to theorize, to construct and think in terms of elaborate symbolic systems. This disposition is very much to the fore in maths and science. Yet this disposition is unintelligible, in any developed form, without a concern for truth, which introduces the aspect of feeling. Anyone who is concerned about getting to the bottom of things must appraise arguments and considerations as cogent, consistent, relevant, etc. which are non-neutral forms of judgment. An important part of the education of the emotions consists in the development of these 'rational passions'.

The separation of intellectual from social development is equally difficult to defend. There is, perhaps, a more widespread tendency to theorize in fields such as philosophy, science and mathematics. But a socially developed person is surely not just one who is a good mixer, who is knowledgeable about social matters, and skilled in how to win friends and influence people; he is also a person who can distance himself a bit from social facts and from his fellows and theorize about them. Intellectuals are sometimes defined denotatively as those who read weeklies such as the *New Statesman*, and *New Society*. Yet these are just the sort of people who would tend to interpret social events in terms of theories about the economic determinants of social change, and the foibles of their friends in terms of some derivative of Freudian theory. Moral development, too, has partly to be understood in terms of the appropriate feelings such as concern for others and a sense of justice, which have an intimate connection with action, and partly in terms of the ability to give depth and breadth to appraisals such as 'wrong' and 'good' by bringing to bear understanding derived from literature, history, and the sciences of man. Thus both social and moral development involve the development of both feeling and the intellect.

Classification of development in terms of modes of experience is not open to objections of the same type. For each mode involves a characteristic cognitive and affective aspect, and development in each will be constituted partly by the degree to which the appropriate appraisals have become part of the individual's outlook and partly by depth and breadth provided by the ability to back this up with theories and the general enlargement of the understanding. Thus the study of Piaget should not be seen just as a study of 'intellectual' and moral development but as providing an important source of material for the better understanding of the scientific, mathematical and moral modes of experience. The study of Freud and his followers should not be thought of as the study of 'emotional development', but of the development of a most crucial form of understanding, namely of other people and ourselves, together with a study of the features of mind and of childhood experience which stunt and distort this form of understanding. This should discourage the tendency, already noted at the start of this chapter, to think dichotomously of educational situations in terms of hard, academic subjects such as maths, science, and history, which have somehow to be mastered, and soft, rather mushy experiences to do with emotions and 'personal relationships', which have to be lived through. For understanding ourselves, and developing emotionally, is just as much a cognitive matter as learning to think scientifically and historically is a matter of developing distinctive feelings and motivations.

So much, then, for the importance of public modes of experience in giving an account of sequential processes of development. Manifestly such a way of conceiving of development does much to reconcile the child-centred with the subject-centred approach to education. But what is to be made of Nagel's third criterion of 'development' at the human level, that of the 'end-state'? Does the cognitive stage theory enable us to say anything about this which is not just an expression of our cultural preferences?

3 The end-state

The notion of an 'end-state', when applied to human development, is a problematic one. Within each mode of experience we can, of course, talk in a provisional way about people being more or less developed, e.g. mathematically, morally, scientifically. In so doing we would be speaking relatively to the standards characterizing the stages which have so far been reached; but it would be rash to say that within any of them a final stage has been reached. But could we go on to say that any content could be given to the notion of 'human development' as applied to man as a person as distinct from in particular forms of development?

We might be inclined to say, using the biological criterion, that a man who had achieved some integration of differentiated forms of experience would be more developed than a man whose consciousness was not so differentiated. Surely, it might be argued, a man who sees the world 'whole' in a way which confuses the scientific and moral notions of lawfulness, is less developed than a post-seventeenth-century man who has distinguished these different forms of lawfulness and who can combine them in a judgment about what ought to be done, e.g. about smoking, in which scientific generalizations are used. Surely, too, we might say that a man whose understanding had progressed a long way in most of the different modes of experience is more developed than a man whose development is confined to one and who has missed out on most of the others. But what sorts of remarks would these be? We might be committed to saying that a man like David Hume, whom we might regard as being reasonably well-developed in this all round sort of way, was more developed as a human being than

Oliver Cromwell, whose consciousness was not very differentiated, or than Gandhi who rather missed out on science and maths. We might say that a polymath was more developed than a disciplined engineer. And these would seem rather bizarre sorts of things to say.

What underlies our feelings of uneasiness about such remarks? It might be argued that 'developed', when used at this level, can never be used purely descriptively; it suggests also some kind of approval. A man can be developed mathematically or scientifically, and this can be related to the standards defining the stages through which people pass. But we still might not value mathematical development very highly, if at all. But, it might be said, when we talk about human development generally this has to be related to some valuative conception of man which is inevitably culture-bound, and which has no universal significance.

This conclusion, however, should not be too quickly drawn; for the stage theory would suggest that certain forms of ideals are only available to people who have progressed to certain stages in the particular modes of development, and that such ideals are not determined by the content of particular cultures. Examples would be ideals such as those of thinking critically, being creative and autonomous. Such ideals would only be attainable by people who had reached a certain level of cognitive development, but they could be exemplified by people who had been brought up with differences in the content of their belief systems and moral codes. It will be remembered that ideals such as these were of importance in the account given of progressive education in the last chapter.

a *Human excellences* Ideals such as these would satisfy the essential condition of being ideals of personal development generally rather than just end-points of development within particular modes of experience; for they refer to human excellences which are extremely important in our concept of 'personal development' because they are intimately connected with what it means to be a 'person'. We can talk of a 'person' in a straightforward non-committal way, as when we say 'He is a pleasant person'. Or we can talk of 'person' in a richer sense as when we demand respect for persons. This use of 'person' is connected conceptually with having what might be called an assertive point of view, with evaluation, decision, and choice, and with being, to a certain extent, an individual who determines his own destiny by his choices. It is concerned, in other words, with the development of reason in its various aspects. Human excellences seem to consist in developing these rational capacities to the full. Critical thought, for instance, is a development of evaluation, autonomy of choice, creativity of the attempt to launch out on one's own and to impose one's own stamp on a product. Integrity is shown in consistency to principles in the face of temptation, and the development of the imagination makes possible fine shades of sensitivity and compassion. These are just examples of excellences that are only possible for someone who has reached a certain level of cognitive development, and they are intimately connected with the development of capacities connected with being a 'person' in this second sense. We often say of someone 'He is a real person'. We are not using this phrase to stress the fact that he is a person in the sense in which any normal human being is. Rather we are drawing attention to the impact which he makes on us in respect of some quality of mind which is intimately connected with the richer sense of being a person – for instance his capacity for imaginative compassion, his independence of mind, or his integrity. In so far, therefore, as we think of someone like Gandhi or Oliver Cromwell as a developed person we think of him as one who has exhibited one or other of these excellences in the sphere to which he has committed himself. He may not be developed in an all round way, but in the sphere to which he has chosen to devote himself he has displayed some excellences which are intimately connected with being a person.

How, then, are these excellences related to the distinct modes of experience in which specific forms of development, such as the mathematical or moral, take place? For there are no general 'powers of the mind' that can be exercised in a vacuum. They are rather adverbial to activities and modes of experience in that they are connected with the manner in which they are conducted. Men can cook, paint, or construct theories creatively; they can feel compassion imaginatively and with great objectivity and integrity; they can be autonomous and critical in their thinking and in their dealings with other men. These excellences are qualities of mind that have to be displayed in specific activities which have their own specific standards, if they are to be distinguished from mere self-expression or contra-suggestibility. It is also the case that particular skills may have to be mastered for these excellences to develop to the full. Nevertheless it does not follow that there is nothing in common between the exercise of these excellences in different spheres. Indeed it would be very strange if it did; for how could the same terms be used intelligibly? A person who is critical, for instance, will not accept what he is told just because he is told it, he will not take authorities too seriously, he will be determined to test things for himself. But different contents can be put into this general formula depending whether the issue is a scientific, philosophical or aesthetic one. The criteria of truth may be different and so may the testing procedures; but 'being critical' can be understood in terms of this general form of proceeding which has a variable content. Of course a given individual may not be very good in all the spheres which he approaches in this way; for he may lack the necessary training and skill. In a similar way we can say that a person is generally intelligent in that he always approaches situations by trying to relate what he is doing to some over-all purpose; but he may lack the skill to bring off what he is trying to do. An intelligent carpenter or golfer may be too unskilled to be a good carpenter or golfer. But meaning can be attached to 'intelligence' in these contexts which does not depend on the specificity of the activities in which a person tries his hand, or on the skill with which he actually performs in them. The same is true of qualities of mind such as being imaginative, critical, and creative.

What does seem to follow, however, is that these general qualities of mind, which have been called excellences, cannot be thought of as general 'powers of the mind' of a person in separation from the modes of experience. Thus personal development is not inconsistent with development in the different modes of experience. On the contrary it presupposes them. These excellences provide, as it were, a kind of H.C.F. of personal development, to use a *façon de parler*, which cuts across the distinct modes of experience. But they can only be exercised in the modes of experience.

b *Personal development and mental health* The same sort of metaphor could also be used to sketch a level of general development as a person which might constitute a kind of L.C.M. Aristotle maintained that man's essence is to be rational and part of what he meant was that, given a normal environment, there is a potentiality in man which will become actual in an ability to use his reason in the sense of planning means to ends and regulating his desires. This is very much what Freud meant by the development of the ego, which he took to give direction to the stages of development. Freud saw clearly that this ability to delay gratification and to plan means to ends is connected with the development of the perceptual apparatus and the working of thought according to the reality principle. Piaget mapped much more carefully what is involved in the development of this basic conception of reality, and the stages at which children develop the forms of thought in which objects are seen in a space-time framework in causal relations with other objects. He also traced how we gradually came to understand actions in terms of taking means to ends, to be aware of others as both similar to and different from ourselves, and to discern intention and purposes immanent in their overtly observable acts. Without concepts such as these the development of reason and of a sense of reality would be inconceivable. And without this our potentiality for becoming persons could not develop.

Now in *any* culture, whatever the group or individual ideal of human development, there is a certain minimum level of functioning that is expected of anyone. The individual has to carry out tasks connected with the household and his occupations; he has to come up to some minimum level of understanding of his environment and other people if he is to be viable in any culture. Indeed, most forms of mental illness can be related to failures in the basic capacities of man as a rational animal which are necessary for carrying out these simple functions. There are, of course, cultures in which mild deviations in these areas are tolerated and even treated with reverential awe; but if an individual is permanently unable to carry out effectively any of his practical purposes, is perpetually hallucinated, schizophrenic, or subject to paranoid delusions, he would be regarded as stunted or deficient in any culture. A strong case can therefore be made for saying that any concept of personal development must include some reference to the rationality of man defined in this minimum sense. This provides the basic form of human experience without which any more idiosyncratic forms of development could not be sustained.

In brief, if we ask the question about the end-state of personal development, as distinct from particular modes of development, it might be possible to produce a very formal account of both an H.C.F. and an L.C.M. of personal development. The latter consists in maintaining the basic structure of man as a rational animal; the former consists in developing these rational capacities to the full. But personal development, as conceived of in these ways, is not distinct from development within the various modes of experience; rather it consists in the development of qualities of mind that are exercised within them. And there may be some qualities of mind, such as wisdom, which consist in being able to draw together considerations taken from different modes of experience, and to bring them to bear on particular problems. We thus have answers to the problems with which we started both about criteria for 'personal development' and of its relationship to more specialized forms of development.

The valuative status of qualities of mind characterizing the 'end-state' has also been made explicit. On the one hand an H.C.F. of human excellences has been distinguished. These are ideals which seem to be connected with the development of reason in its various aspects. On the other hand there is an L.C.M. of mental health. This is a level of rational functioning which is a *sine qua non* of any form of personal development. So value must be accorded to the rationality of man, even if defined in this minimal sense, as a precondition of any form of personal development. Nothing, however, has been said about the *justification* of those qualities of mind that have been termed human excellences. This is consistent with the plan of this book. For, as was indicated at the end of the last chapter, the analysis here presented gives rise to further questions which must be pursued in other branches of philosophy.

4 Development and education

There is, however, an interesting further question which arises from this analysis of 'development' and which does not require entry into another branch of philosophy in order to tackle it. It is this: if we leave aside physical development, is the concept of 'human development' much different from that of the specific concept of 'education'? In the old days when theories of development were mainly maturational theories which stressed inner ripening, and when education was much more closely associated with instruction, training, and various forms of 'stamping in' procedures, there was an obvious contrast. But nowadays almost no one of any repute is prepared to defend a maturational type of theory of mental development, and in educational theory there is a constant controversy between those who stress 'leading out' and those who stress instruction and training. There is, therefore, little to distinguish controversies about factors which determine human development from those about appropriate educational procedures.

There seems, therefore, to be little difference between 'education' and 'development' in relation to the second criterion of 'development', that of sequential change. The first criterion of pre-existing structure has not been treated as being of any great significance. The difference, therefore, if there is any, between the two concepts, is likely to be connected with the third criterion of the 'end-state'. Is there any difference?

It has been suggested (see Ch. 2) that in so far as we are concerned with educating people, in the specific sense of 'educate', we are concerned with bringing about desirable states of mind in people characterized by some depth and breadth of understanding. Aims of education, it was argued, specify in more detail what these desirable states of mind are thought to be. So human excellences such as autonomy, creativeness, integrity could surely be regarded as aims of education as well as culminating points of development. They would manifestly satisfy the desirability condition of 'being educated'. But would they necessarily satisfy the knowledge conditions as well? Surely not necessarily; for a man could display such excellences and lack breadth of understanding. Not all human excellences are the prerogative of educated men, though some of them, such as critical thought, probably are. Thus the integrity or autonomy of an educated man would be of rather a different order from that of an uneducated one because of the presence or absence of all-round understanding. This difference between an educated man and being a developed person is reflected in the way in which we use the expressions. For, as has already been observed, we might well say that Gandhi or Gauguin were developed human beings because they displayed some human excellence; but they would not necessarily be educated men. The fact that they personified some human excellence would be sufficient to describe them as developed human beings without further questions being asked about their all-round understanding. But such further questions would have to be pressed before we would be prepared to describe them as educated men as well. Conversely we might describe a person as an educated man even if he did not display any human excellence. He might have achieved a fair mastery of the different modes of experience without having developed any human excellences in them. He might live a life that was morally impeccable, have a developed aesthetic sense, and understand the second law of thermodynamics as well as the causes of the decline of Roman civilization. He might be sensitive in his personal relationships and be not without some kind of religious awe at man's predicament in the universe – a quiet man, working at a humble job, living in a suburb in which he cultivated his garden with love and a sound understanding of the nicer points of horticulture.

These suggestions about the difference between being an educated man and being developed as a person are very speculative and should not be taken too seriously. There are obviously differences between the concepts that it might be interesting to explore; but neither of the two concepts are sufficiently determinate for much to be said which would command universal agreement. As has been pointed out many times before, nothing ultimately depends on such analysis. It is only a useful technique for getting clearer about possible similarities and differences which may be of importance in some contexts. But what does emerge clearly from this analysis is that the concept of 'human development', like that of 'education', is inescapably valuative. Some ideal conception of a human being is presupposed. A teacher of progressive persuasion, therefore, who demands that the content and manner of teaching must be closely related to facts of human development cannot proceed purely on the basis of empirical facts. For his selection can only be made in the light of some ethical view about what qualities of mind are constitutive of human development. His biological approach to his task, therefore, only provides stimulating analogies. In the end he, like any other teacher, has to make up his mind about valuative issues.

The other important point that has emerged from this analysis of 'human development' is the central role played by what we have called public modes of experience. Reference to these was necessary in giving an account not only of the various facets of human development but also of the elusive notion of development as a 'person'. It is now time to examine the features of such modes of experience in more detail and to enquire into how they are related to the curriculum.

4
The curriculum

Introduction

The last two chapters have brought to the fore two of the logical demands that all adequately planned educational practice must face. First there is the inescapable matter of determining somehow the aims, ends or objectives of the enterprise. Secondly there is the crucial point that if we examine carefully the character of the central objectives sought by progressives, we find that they, as much as those sought by traditionalists, are necessarily related to the acquisition of certain fundamental forms of what we have loosely called public modes of experience, understanding and knowledge.

As has already been indicated it is not the purpose of this book to pursue the first of these demands further. That education necessitates decisions of this kind is a philosophical point. The actual decisions themselves are, however, not properly made by attending to philosophical considerations only. Psychological, social, economic and other factors are equally important. Yet the relevant philosophical considerations are precisely our concern and the second demand that has emerged is of this kind. Its significance will, therefore, now be pursued further within the more specific context of curriculum planning.

1 Curriculum objectives

a *The need for objectives* We shall take the term 'curriculum' to be the label for a programme or course of activities which is explicitly organized as the means whereby pupils may attain the desired objectives, whatever these may be. In keeping with the earlier argument, the planning of a curriculum, or any part of it, is here seen as a logical nonsense until the objectives being aimed at are made clear. At this level general statements of aims have to be translated into statements of specific objectives to which curriculum activities can be explicitly directed. Such specification is far from easy and, as yet, no universal categories in which to carry it out are agreed. The celebrated *Taxonomy of Educational Objectives* by B. S. Bloom and his colleagues, two volumes of which have so far appeared, is an important first attempt at a comprehensive scheme. It divides the whole area into cognitive, affective and psycho-motor domains, endeavouring to list classes of detailed objectives that might be pursued in each. In the cognitive domain, for instance, the categorization lists knowledge of specific items of information, of terminologies, conventions, classifications and generalizations. Different types of intellectual abilities and skills are distinguished. In the affective domain there are, for instance, classes of different types of dispositions to respond, ranging from mere acquiescence to enjoyment, and classes of types of valuing. But valuable though this attempt may be in certain respects, it shows no awareness of the fundamental, necessary relationships between the various kinds of objectives that can be distinguished. A knowledge of the meaning of terms can certainly be thought of as in a different category from a knowledge of empirical facts or an acceptance of a rule of behaviour. But clearly, in any given case, an achievement in one of these categories might be interrelated, even necessarily, with achievements in the others. Much knowledge of facts about, say, the weather, presupposes a knowledge of the meaning of appropriate terms; and accepting certain rules of behaviour might be justifiable only on a basis of such facts. Thus when it comes to deciding the curriculum objectives which we wish to pursue, we cannot behave as though they are independent elements that can even be characterized, let alone achieved, in isolation from each other. And to say this is but to put in another form what has been argued in Ch. 3 about the nature of those desirable states of mind with which education in its specific sense is centrally concerned, that fundamental to all these, are those distinct, public modes of experience and knowledge which man has now achieved. What we need for satisfactory curriculum planning, then, is a grasp of the structure or pattern of relationships there is between the objectives in which we are interested. Mapping objectives in this way is an immensely complex philosophical task demanding much detailed analytical work in epistemology and the philosophy of mind. Little of this has as yet been done. Yet from the work there is, one or two tentative general conclusions can be drawn about this structure that are clearly of great importance for curriculum decisions.

It has been argued that underlying all the more sophisticated objectives such as autonomy, creativeness and critical thought, there must necessarily be the achievements of objective experience, knowledge and understanding. If this is so it suggests that the logically most fundamental objectives of all are those of a cognitive kind, on the basis of which, out of which, or in relation to which, all others must be developed. For only in so far as one has the relevant knowledge and forms of reasoning can a person be creative or critical in, say, atomic physics. Only in so far as one understands other people can one come to care about them and actively seek their good. Enjoying and valuing the arts is impossible without the concepts that make aesthetic experience available. The fundamental structure of the objectives would therefore seem to be within the domain of objective experience and knowledge. If we can map the relationships of achievements here, there is hope that we might eventually progress to a grasp of the more complex pattern of the elements built on these. What, then, are the basic achievements that are necessary to objective experience and knowledge and what structure does there seem to be within this domain?

b *Modes of knowledge and experience* Let us begin by noting that there can be no experience or knowledge without the acquisition of the relevant concepts. Further, it is only when experience and thought, which necessarily involve the use of concepts of some sort, involve those shared in a public world, that the achievements with which we are concerned are possible. Without shared concepts there can be no such distinctions as those between fact and fantasy, truth and error. Only where there is public agreement about the classification and categorization of experience and thought can we hope for any objectivity within them. But merely shared concepts are insufficient for what we mean by objectivity. Connected with these concepts must be objective tests for what it is claimed is experienced, known or understood. Such tests are perhaps best exemplified by the tests of observation in the sciences, though there would seem to be no good reason for considering science to be the only objective pursuit. The crucial point is that, though objective judgments are not possible without a body of agreed concepts, the judgments themselves are not matters of further agreement. It is only because we agree on the meanings of the words employed that we can understand the claim that over five million people live in the Greater London area. Whether or not that claim is true is, however, not a matter of further agreement, but of objective test. Any agreement there may be amongst us about this claim is not just a matter of our deciding but is properly thrust on us by what is the case. And that remains true whether we are concerned with what is the case about the world, God, a work of art or a moral action. It is, therefore, only through the mastery of a body of public concepts, with their related objective tests, that objective experience and knowledge can be achieved. And if this is so, then the basic structure of objectives we are after must be one within that body of concepts and related tests which man has so far developed.

In looking for this structure it is not appropriate here to discuss the detail of relations between the particular concepts which we might wish to teach; for we are concerned only with the more general features of these relations that are significant for overall curriculum planning. What we really want to know at this general level is whether the domain of objective experience and knowledge is, for example, one complex body of interrelated concepts, a unity of some sort, a number of similar forms of experience and knowledge with parallel relations between the concepts in each area, or whether it has some other implicit organization. To answer this question necessitates an examination of the conceptual relations embedded in the many forms of public expression we have and of the serious claims to objective tests that are associated with these. An examination of this scope cannot be undertaken here; for this we must refer the reader elsewhere. Much of the work in this area is controversial, yet it seems to us to indicate a differentiation of modes of experience and knowledge that are fundamentally different in character.

Detailed studies suggest that some seven areas can be distinguished, each of which necessarily involves the use of concepts of a particular kind and a distinctive type of test for its objective claims. The truths of formal logic and mathematics involve concepts that pick out relations of a general abstract kind, where deducibility within an axiom system is the particular test for truth. The physical sciences, on the other hand, are concerned with truths that, in the last analysis, stand or fall by the tests of observation by the senses. Abstract though the theoretical concepts they employ may be, the sciences necessarily employ concepts for what is seen, heard, felt, touched or smelt; for it is with an understanding and knowledge of the sensible world that they are concerned. To be clearly distinguished from knowledge and experience of the physical world is our awareness and understanding of our own and other people's minds. Concepts like those of 'believing', 'deciding', 'intending', 'wanting', 'acting', 'hoping' and 'enjoying', which are essential to inter-personal experience and knowledge, do not pick out, in any straightforward way, what is observable by the senses. Indeed the phrase 'knowledge without observation' has been coined to make this point. The precise nature of the grounds of our objective judgments in this area is not yet adequately understood, though their irreducibility to other types of test can perhaps be most readily seen in judgments of our own states of mind. Moral judgment and awareness necessitate, in their turn, another family of concepts such as 'ought', 'wrong' and 'duty'. Unless actions or states are understood in such terms, it is not their moral character of which we are aware. The claim to objectivity in the case of moral judgments is a matter of long-standing dispute, but the sustained attempts there have been to show the objectivity of morals, and its irreducibility to other forms of knowledge, make this domain one which must be recognized as having serious claims to independent status. Likewise the claims for a distinctive mode of objective aesthetic experience, using forms of symbolic expression not confined to the linguistic, must be taken seriously, even though much philosophical work remains to be done here. Religious claims in their traditional forms certainly make use of concepts which, it is now maintained, are irreducible in character. Whether or not there are objective grounds for what is asserted is again a matter on which much more has yet to be said. The case would certainly seem to be one that cannot be simply dismissed. Finally philosophical understanding, as indicated in Ch. 1, would seem to involve unique second order concepts and forms of objective tests irreducible to those of any first order kind.

The differentiation of these seven areas is based on the claim that in the last analysis, all our concepts seem to belong to one of a number of distinct, if related, categories which philosophical analysis is concerned to clarify. These categories are marked out in each case by certain fundamental, ultimate or categoreal concepts of a most general kind which other concepts in the category presuppose. It will be remembered that the difference between the 'form' and 'content' of experience was held, in Ch. 3, to be of crucial importance in giving an account of the development of modes of experience. It is these categoreal concepts that provide the form of experience in the different modes. Our understanding of the physical world, for instance, involves such categoreal concepts as those of 'space', 'time' and 'cause'. Concepts such as those of 'acid', 'electron' and 'velocity', all presuppose these categoreal notions. In the religious domain, the concept of 'God' or 'the transcendent' is presumably categoreal whereas the concept of 'prayer' operates at a lower level. In the moral area the term 'ought' labels a concept of categoreal status, as the term 'intention' would seem to do in our understanding of persons. The distinctive type of objective test that is necessary to each domain is clearly linked with the meaning of these categoreal terms, though the specific forms the tests take may depend on the lower level concepts employed. This can be seen especially in the different sciences, different tests all presupposing the same categoreal notions.

The division of modes of experience and knowledge suggested

here is thus a fundamental categoreal division, based on the range of such irreducible categories which we at present seem to have. That other domains might, in due course, come to be distinguished, is in no sense being prejudged; for the history of human consciousness would seem to be one of progressive differentiation. The categorization that is at present being suggested may in fact be inaccurate in detail. Be that as it may. What we are suggesting is that within the domain of objective experience and knowledge, there are such radical differences of kind that experience and knowledge of one form is neither equatable with, nor reducible to, that of any other form. In each case it is only by a grasp of the appropriate concepts and tests that experience and knowledge of that kind become available to the individual. Achievements in one domain must be recognized as radically different from those in any other. What is more, within any one domain the concepts used, and the objective claims made, form a particular network of relations. In some cases concepts are tightly connected in a pattern of necessary dependence. In others the relations are more complex and difficult to specify. The forms of justification likewise differ. Thus the concepts and claims of the domain can only be grasped in their varied relations to each other.

But the radical independence which each of these modes has in relation to the others, is only one aspect of the situation. What is also important is the pattern of interrelationships between them. On a moment's reflection it can immediately be seen that, however independent the domain of science may be, our understanding of the physical world is tightly dependent on our mathematical knowledge. It is also a commonplace that scientific discoveries involve us in new moral dilemmas. Equally some religious claims presuppose historical truths, whilst others demand moral understanding. Yet these interrelations must not be thought to weaken in any way the claims for independence made above. That experience or knowledge in one domain is *necessary* to that of another in no way implies that it is *sufficient*. Of itself no amount of mathematical knowledge is sufficient for solving a scientific problem, nor is science alone able to provide moral understanding. What we must recognize is that the development of knowledge and experience in one domain may be impossible without the use of elements of understanding and awareness from some other. But even when incorporated into another domain these elements retain their own unique character and validity. The observable features of an event remain such, no matter what religious interpretation may be offered of it. That an appeal to certain empirical facts may be necessary to justifying a moral principle means that there is a scientific prerequisite for moral understanding in this case. But that prerequisite must be judged by appropriate scientific canons and its establishment is independent of the moral principle under consideration. And, granted the scientific truth, its significance for the moral principle can be judged only by moral canons. At this point the scientific canons now become irrelevant. It thus seems that the form of interrelationship between the independent domains of knowledge and experience can only be properly understood by recognizing first the basic differences between them, and then by seeing how they are interlocked when one domain employs elements of another without any loss to the independent character of each.

c *The selection of objectives* The fundamental structural relations, which have been briefly sketched, have numerous implications for the choice of educational objectives to be served by a curriculum. Foremost among these is the fact that, if education is understood as developing desirable states of mind characterized by knowledge and understanding, we must decide with which of the several fundamentally different types of knowledge and understanding we are concerned. To educate a person significantly in some of these only is to limit the forms of his development which we are prepared systematically to pursue. The issue of breadth in education as opposed to narrow specialization is, if faced properly, surely the issue of whether or not a person is being significantly introduced to each of the fundamentally different types of objective experience and knowledge that are open to men. Not to try to introduce pupils to certain areas, or to give up too soon when the going becomes hard, is to accept that in these areas the individual shall, as far as the school is concerned, develop no further. Admittedly what can be achieved in any area is a matter of degree. Yet experience would suggest that, only after sustained attention to the relevant concepts, the patterns of reasoning and tests for judgment peculiar to any domain, do these elements of thought function spontaneously in a clear and coherent way. It is therefore not surprising that there is a persistent call that general education shall be maintained for all throughout the secondary school stage.

The adequate development of general education has not only suffered from a lack of clarity about the range of understanding and knowledge it should pursue. It has also suffered from a failure to distinguish between the precise objectives of general education and those of special education within the same domain of knowledge and experience. A budding specialist needs a detailed knowledge of all the relevant concepts, skills and tests for truth that will progressively provide him with a comprehensive understanding within a given domain. In this area his knowledge and experience will eventually stretch far beyond the confines of everyday contexts. A general education, however, aims at no such exhaustive mastery. Its concern is that the pupil will be sufficiently immersed in each form of understanding to appreciate its character, to employ its major elements that have application within the context of everyday life, and to be aware of the further possibilities in each area, given the time and inclination to pursue these. Clearly there can be an endless variety of courses in any area, the concern of which is a blend of these two. What we need, however, is undoubtedly the working out of the detailed objectives for courses say in English literature, which are appropriate on the one hand for the sixteen-year-old school leaver of average ability, and on the other for the sixteen-year-old 'O' Level candidate who may or may not be going to specialize further in this domain. Equally we need them for the eighteen-year-old entrant to engineering studies at a polytechnic and for the eighteen-year-old university entrance scholar in English literature.

We have been at pains to emphasize, on philosophical grounds, the significance for the pupil's development of choosing certain educational objectives rather than others. By our choice of objectives we are deciding how far his scientific, aesthetic or religious development is or is not important. In making the choice, however, it must not be forgotten, as was mentioned at the outset, that there are legitimate social demands for specific objectives that intelligent planning cannot ignore. A degree of specialized knowledge and skill in some limited area may be a necessity for all of us, for the good of the whole community as much as for our own individual good. At the present time, the balance of forms of specialist training needed in our own society is as yet little more than a matter of speculation. Our choice must also take into account the relevant psychological knowledge we have of human abilities and motivation to learn. Just how far we are, at will, able to determine the pattern of development of any one individual, given our present methods of teaching and upbringing, is a controversial question. Certainly at present not everyone could be turned into a Newton or an Einstein, try as best we might. A rationally defensible curriculum must be planned to reach objectives that are defensible and that not only from a philosophical point of view. Philosophy can seek to outline the nature and interrelation of objectives, thus indicating what coherent selection necessitates. It can indicate, too, the significance in human development of certain choices. It cannot go further alone.

2 Curriculum organization

a *The means-ends model* Once granted a set of desired objectives, diverse in their character and complex in their interrelations, the business of curriculum planning becomes the organization of the best means to achieve these ends. Yet expressed in this way the situation is liable to be misunderstood. For though the means/ends model brings out well that, logically, the objectives must be determined before all else, it is often taken to imply that no particular means are logically necessary for reaching the stated ends, and that the ends and the means can be characterized in complete independence of each other. A fountain pen may be the means whereby a certain shape is drawn on a piece of paper, but clearly quite other means could be used, and the shape outlined has no significant connection of a logical sort with the nature of the fountain pen used. But in the case of the curriculum, looked at from one point of view, the means employed may be, and often are, closely interrelated with the ends. Only if one understands how to solve certain types of algebraic equations can problems about planetary motion be solved by Newtonian mechanics. Learning the algebraic techniques can therefore harmlessly be regarded as a means to an understanding of planetary motion. But it is not one of many alternative means here, the best of which could be decided by empirical investigation. A grasp of Newtonian mechanics logically necessitates an understanding of these equations. The means and the end are here inseparably connected so that the latter is not even characterizable without appeal to the former. Indeed, in many cases the means to certain ultimate objectives can be broken down into the achieving of a series of subordinate but necessary objectives, which may be both valuable objectives in themselves and even logically necessary to the achievement of the ultimate objectives. Up to a point the interrelations between objectives can necessitate a certain sequence within the curriculum.

Looked at from another point of view, the means to the curriculum's objectives consists of a programme of activities specifically selected and organized to bring about the forms of development that are desired. The distinctive character of these educational activities will be discussed in the next chapter. But of interest at this juncture, because of its close connection with the structure of objectives we have outlined, is the type of units which curriculum organization may involve.

b *The nature of school 'subjects'* Clearly any realistic attempt to achieve objectives of the variety and complexity pursued in modern education, must somehow break the enterprise down into a number of limited tasks of manageable proportions. Traditionally this has been done by organizing the curriculum into so-called school 'subjects' such as arithmetic, history, English, R.E., and woodwork. Under each of these headings a limited range of objectives is pursued to the exclusion of all others, and activities particularly appropriate for these ends are planned within each unit. Regular periods of time are usually allotted to these activities according to the importance attached to the objectives in each case. But on what principle are these units constructed? Is there any reason to think that this is the only, or even the best way of organizing learning? It is tempting to try to defend this organization on the ground that it, and it alone, is based on the radical differences which we have been concerned to bring out between distinct independent modes of objective experience and knowledge. On examining a typical list of subjects, however, it is obvious that they do not by any means all pursue a group of objectives within one such mode. Under English, or geography, or R.E. several types of understanding may be sought at once. And this simple fact brings to the fore the important point that curriculum units, whatever their character may be, subject, topic, project or some other, must be seen as units constructed simply for educational purposes. They have no ultimate value outside this context. Because our experience and knowledge is differentiated into a number of distinct forms it does not at all follow that the best way of developing such knowledge and experience is to organize a curriculum in terms of these forms. There may be many psychological factors about learning and motivation which would argue against such a pattern. Social demands on the curriculum may make it desirable to bring together knowledge and understanding from different modes. On philosophical grounds alone, any curriculum composed of subjects, each structured to objectives within one mode, would do scant justice to the complex interrelations between the modes that have already been pointed out. Developing a person's knowledge and experience necessarily involves developing these in the different modes, but that does not mean that one must concern oneself with each of these separately in isolation from all others. All understanding of moral problems does not have to be pursued in a context devoid of any concern for aesthetic appreciation, just because the two modes are of radically different kinds. The two can indeed both be developed, at least in part, by the use of certain works of English literature.

The process of developing different forms of distinct yet interrelated experience and understanding can be likened to building a jigsaw. One procedure with a jigsaw might be to structure the enterprise by attending in turn to patches of different colours; so one might attend to particular independent modes of experience within a curriculum. But there is no necessity to do so. One might equally compose the jigsaw by attending to the outlines of different objects and characters drawn on the surface, no matter what colours are involved. One might instead, at least in the early stages, begin by placing the pieces that form the outer edges. In fact there are many different systematic procedures for building a jigsaw, all of which, however, result in the same interlocked and structured achievement. The same is true with the curriculum. Quite different types of curriculum unit may be used but, if they are effective, they will all necessarily result in the progressive achievement of the structured set of objectives that are desired. In any effective procedure, just as the coloured patches must necessarily be composed in the jigsaw, so the independent modes of understanding and experience must be built from the necessary interlocking elements in the curriculum. It therefore seems that, though the objectives, in which we are interested, must be seen to be related to each other in a structure of independent modes of experience and knowledge, it is possible to pursue these ends within a variety of curriculum units. Certain units might be devoted to objectives within a single mode, as for instance in the study of arithmetic. Others, as in the case of a subject like geography, or in a project, say on local industry, may be concerned with objectives taken from several different modes.

Yet if what matters is that the desired objectives be reached in their interrelated structure, though there may be no one universal way of achieving these, it would seem likely that there are some restrictions on the design of effective curriculum units which will spring from the nature of the structure which is to be built. It is, after all, perfectly possible to think of systematic ways of approaching a jigsaw which would in fact never succeed in fitting it together. One might, for instance, try to place all the pieces having an area of one square inch first, then move on to those with an area of 1·2 square inches and so on. In curriculum planning one might try to produce units by grouping together objectives in ways that pay no attention to the other objectives with which they are necessarily interrelated. The strength of units devoted to a single mode of experience and knowledge is that they permit systematic attention to be given to the progressive mastery of closely interrelated concepts, patterns of reasoning and qualities of mind, by radically restricting the character of the objectives with which they are concerned. Although elements from other modes may be used within such 'subjects', the mastery of these is assumed to have been dealt with elsewhere. Such units, of course, stress the independence of the different modes.

c *Curriculum integration* The more well established subjects which are concerned with objectives of more than one mode, as, say, geography or English, have unusually been relatively restricted in the range of modes involved. In recent years, however, there has been pressure for them to extend their interests ever wider. Under the label of English, for instance, it is now not uncommon to find concern for an understanding of other persons and of moral matters, as much as aesthetic and linguistic elements. Such subjects have become important in emphasizing the connections which exist between different independent domains. The problem with them has always been that of developing adequately a mastery of elements within the several quite different types of experience and knowledge concerned, without sustained and systematic attention to these individually. Not surprisingly, when effectively pursued, they have repeatedly broken down into the distinct study of different aspects belonging to the various modes involved. This problem becomes acute, if not insuperable, with the topic or project type of curriculum unit where objectives from many modes are brought together. Where the objectives can be effectively reached by these means, and where the interrelation between those, which the topic or project pursues, is genuine and not artificial, such units have an important function.

Yet, to be successful, such work necessarily makes vast demands on the knowledge and ability of the teachers involved. In less competent hands, project and topic work can only too easily degenerate into pursuits which, however interesting, have little or no educational value. If the objectives from the different domains are not being adequately related to the structures within each of these, little is likely to be achieved. If the objectives grouped together have no significant relationship to each other, there seems little point to this exercise, which serves only to draw attention away from the necessary interrelations which objectives necessarily have within the separate modes. One wonders what is gained by organizing a project on hands concerned with physiology, the conditions of employment of factory hands, and the religious significance of the laying on of hands. Above all there would seem to be an ever present danger that this form of curriculum organization be allowed to determine what educational objectives it shall serve. A topic or project that provides an excellent way into learning elements within one of the modes, is of no wider educational value if the only elements of other modes with which it is significantly related are either known already, or are of little educational importance, or are inappropriate for pupils at this stage. There would seem to be something seriously wrong with any form of education in which the organization of the means becomes more important than the ends it serves.

Yet, if a doctrinaire insistence on integrated curriculum units may be seriously miseducative, such units nevertheless would seem to have a crucial place in really adequate curriculum planning. The traditional subject curriculum has, both in complex subjects like geography and general science, and in attempts at keeping in step interrelated subjects like mathematics and physics, at times gone some way to prevent an artificial isolation of certain domains. What it has not been able to do so successfully, however, is adequately to plan for those educational objectives which of their logical nature demand an integrated approach. This is most conspicuously the case if we think of the demands of adequate education in the making of practical, and especially moral, judgments. Judgments as to what ought to be done in personal and social affairs can only be validly made on the basis of a great deal of knowledge – of the physical world, of society, of the interests and feelings of other people, of the principles on which objective moral judgment must rest. Even efficiency judgments in everyday life, as well as in technical situations, can demand attention to many different factors. Adequate education in this area thus needs, at the very least, to develop the ability to recognize the relevance of very diverse considerations in these cases, and the ability to bring them together in a responsible practical judgment. These are clearly not easy to develop, but what is of importance in this context is that such education necessarily demands an integration of knowledge and understanding from many of the different domains. This being so, it is hard to see how the use of topics and projects can possibly here be avoided. If, in addition to the making of judgments, the related practical arts and skills for carrying out the decisions are also accepted as objectives, the argument for having both topics and projects in the curriculum would seem to be conclusive.

The issue of whether or not a curriculum should be composed solely of independent subjects or of other, integrated units, is thus not simply one of the most effective and efficient means of teaching and learning in areas where both approaches are possible. Clearly integrated units, simply by virtue of their complexity, can be the means of much valuable learning of many different kinds and from a motivational point of view may have much to recommend them. Yet behind this level of discussion lie considerations of the nature of the objectives being aimed at. Just as it is hard to see how the distinctive character of logically distinct modes of knowledge and experience can possibly be understood without some separate systematic attention to them, so it is hard to see how, without the use of properly designed integrative units, the complex interrelations of the domains can be adequately appreciated. The unfortunate polarization of curriculum debate into an opposition between the 'traditional' devotees of subjects and the 'progressive' devotees of integration, can here, as elsewhere, be seen to rest, at least in part, on philosophical misunderstandings on both sides. The nature of educational objectives demands that adequate attention be paid to developing systematically the pupil's grasp of modes of experience and knowledge which are both independent and yet intimately interrelated. To fail to attend to either of these aspects by sheer oversight, or in the name of some ill-considered theory of the unity of knowledge, is to distort the whole enterprise.

In discussing the organization of the curriculum we have confined ourselves to the nature of the units formed by grouping objectives. Such units would seem to be a practical necessity in all curriculum planning. Just how such units might be employed has not, however, been considered. Traditionally 40-45 minute periods have been allotted to different subjects. Yet clearly it is sometimes possible to do away with such an arrangement, leaving the detailed allocation of time to individual teachers or to individual pupils. The curriculum units employed in an 'integrated day' may in fact be as subject structured as those in the most traditional grammar-school curriculum. Changes in curricula are not always quite what they seem at first sight. This is equally true in another respect; for calls for the integration of the curriculum are not infrequently confused with calls for the introduction of new types of learning and teaching activity. Indeed it is important to recognize that, at times, we are asked to accept a quite unnecessary package deal, which links an organization of curriculum units with the introduction of new teaching methods. But whether the units of a curriculum are subjects based on independent modes of experience and knowledge, or subjects concerned with several such modes, or topics of some kind, or combinations of all these, it is equally possible to use the widest variety of modern methods. Team-teaching, individual and group discussion work, the use of teaching machines, films, visits and chalk and talk, these and all others can be used equally with a subject structured curriculum as with any other. In rational curriculum planning questions about the structure of the curriculum must be kept clearly distinct from questions about the best activities and methods to be used. About the latter we have so far said practically nothing. To the distinctive character of educational activities we must now turn our attention.

5
Teaching

Introduction

Although thus far we have concentrated almost exclusively on the ends of 'education', both in general terms and in the context of curriculum planning, it was pointed out earlier that the term 'education' is as frequently used to label the activities that serve these ends as it is to label the ends themselves. We must now therefore consider what distinguishes activities as educational, and how they are to be understood as contributing to the ends already discussed.

On even the most superficial reflection it can readily be seen that 'educating' is not a single specific activity or process like gargling or cycling. The term seems rather to cover a family of activities much as the term 'gardening' does. If a person is described as gardening he may be either digging, or hoeing, or pruning, and so on. Which he is doing at any one time is not specified; but he must be doing one of these; for gardening does not exist apart from them. 'Education' is similar in this respect, though it seems to be an even more abstract term. We say quite naturally that we spent the morning gardening or cooking, but it seems odd to say we spent it educating, or to say 'Go and get on with your educating'. 'Educate' like 'reform', 'improve', 'ameliorate' and other such words, seems to draw attention only to the standards to which the class of activities must conform and which give them their principle of unity. We therefore have a group of activities related at this very high level in that they all contribute somehow to achieving the general end of an educated person.

1 The concept of 'learning'

a *Mastery* Is this all that characterizes the processes of education, or can anything more be said? At least one thing can, namely that the processes must involve learning. Changes brought about by natural physiological or maturational processes, for instance,

74

however desirable they might be, would not be described as education. But this is merely to instance what education and learning are not, when what we need are more positive characteristics. Difficult though the matter is, two features, at least, seem to be logically necessary conditions of learning and hence of education. First learning always has an object. One is necessarily learning a particular X and the process is therefore always related to some kind of mastery of X, to a particular success or achievement. To have learnt, is always to have come up to some standard: for example to know what previously one did not know, or to have mastered a given skill. The kinds of possible achievement here are at least as varied as the kinds of objectives we instanced in the last chapter, and it is therefore not surprising if the particular forms that learning takes are equally varied. Reading, reciting, watching, drawing, making an endless variety of physical movements, are all amongst the more obvious learning activities. Indeed the possibilities would seem to be endless; for is there any activity that could not be part of learning something?

b *Experience* Mastery is, however, not sufficient to distinguish learning, as we clearly must exclude the forms of maturation mentioned earlier. It is also at least theoretically possible for people to be born knowing certain things or equipped with certain skills, and these we would not describe as learnt. What we seem to demand here is that the mastery, or the achievement, be the product of the person's own past experience. In saying this, however, it must be recognized that the learning might occur without the person's being explicitly aware of the particular form of mastery he has achieved. Still, the change of state could have occurred through experience of some sort. But if we insist on experience, are we to insist on conscious awareness at all? What about sleep learning, or the theoretical possibility of acquiring knowledge through the influence of drugs? And if we are not to insist on conscious awareness, what about the differences between, on the one hand, processes which present the material to be learnt as if one were conscious, as in the case of sleep learning or hypnotism, and on the other the possible use of drugs, where this is not the case? Psychologists tend to use the term 'learning' to cover any change in behaviour that is not the product of maturation. Thus a psychologist might include under 'learning' changes in behaviour brought about by drugs, which manifestly are not changes brought about through the influence of experience; he would also include changes brought about through subliminal 'experiences' and through various forms of positive and negative reinforcement of which the learner was not consciously aware. Whether or not 'learning' is to be used in this wide sense or in the narrower sense, which picks out some kind of conscious experience which leads on to some appropriate achievement, is a matter for decision. In a sense it does not much matter which use is preferred provided that the differences are appreciated and provided that it is not thought that there must be some general principles of learning that cover all these different uses. The decision will depend on the distinctions which it is thought important to make in a given context. For our purposes at the moment we shall not pursue this matter further. We propose to follow the general use of the term 'learning', which still, for most of us who are not psychologists, suggests some form of conscious or non-conscious experience which is thought to be necessary to the achievement involved. That certainly leaves the door wide open to the making of finer distinctions within that use, which many may consider important when one turns to learning in an educational context.

c *Education and learning* Granted this, it must be noted that if all educational processes are processes of learning, not all processes of learning are processes of education. The value criterion for education clearly implies that much which can be learnt must be excluded from education either as undesirable, for instance a sexual perversion, or as trivial, for instance wiggling one's ears. And with such achievements rejected, activities which result in these are thereby rejected also, unless of course the same activities can produce other more valuable overriding, and educationally desirable, ends. To the processes themselves, however, irrespective of any achievements in which they might result, there might be objections; for the value criterion of 'education' would seem to apply to judgments on the processes as well as to judgments about their outcomes. For this reason, if for no other, certain processes of learning in general, might not be acceptable as forms of 'educational' learning. An example might be a process that involved lack of respect for learners as persons.

2 *The concept of 'teaching'*

a *Education and teaching* Usually educational processes involve not only learning, but teaching as well. There is, however, no logical connection in this case. Education can go on without any teaching. We can say it was a 'real education' for someone to take a boat out on his own, implying that he learnt something desirable without anybody having been there to ram home the lesson. There are many forms of learning that go on without teaching, and 'educative' learning does not imply the additional criterion that the learning must take place in a teaching situation. It may be a general empirical fact that most things are learnt more rapidly and more reliably if the situation is explicity structured by a teacher. But it certainly is not a conceptual truth that either 'learning' or 'education' implies 'teaching'.

The contemporary concern in education for learning rather than teaching clearly has behind it the important principle that learning is logically necessary to education, whereas teaching is not. Yet much serious miseducation can result if too much attention is paid to this point, at the expense of what is, as a matter of empirical fact, necessary to pupils learning the desired objectives. Indeed it is simply because of the practical impossibility that many of these objectives will ever be attained without teaching, that it is important for us to be clear about the nature of that activity. It was argued earlier that the concepts and types of test for truth within the different forms of objective experience are central educational objectives. These, and the related qualities of mind in which we are interested, have only become possible to us through the progressive elaboration of complex linguistic structures, social institutions, and traditions, built up over thousands of years. And they are open to each child individually only by mastery of the complex non-natural world in which they are embedded. The abstract nature and complex structure of these objectives is such that the only way in which it would seem possible for youngsters to acquire these efficiently and effectively, is for us to introduce pupils to them deliberately and systematically. The notion that by simply living in, and exploring freely, even their social as well as their material context, pupils could acquire the sophisticated, rule-governed principles and procedures we wish them to acquire, for instance when things are correct or incorrect, valid or invalid etc., would be laughable if it were not so frequently assumed. To act in this way deliberately, or for want of adequate planning, shows a total lack of comprehension of the complex nature of the objectives, and the little that most of us can achieve unaided in either thought or action.

It seems, then, that many of the things we want pupils to learn we must deliberately and systematically teach, and it is surely the central function of schools to carry out this task. If that is so, though teaching may not be necessary to all forms of education and learning, it is necessary to schooling. And those elements of education and learning, with which the school is concerned, are intentionally planned, both in objectives and learning activities, by teachers and others in authority. Institutions which are not in some sense deliberately concerned with teaching, however unusual their methods, would hardly seem to deserve the title of school;

and where institutions desert this function for others, however desirable in themselves, one might well ask who is now accepting the responsibility for doing something deliberately about the pupils' learning.

b *The intention to bring about learning* But what characterizes teaching, and how are we to distinguish its activities? As in the cases of learning and gardening, there is again no one specific activity being labelled. Yet one common feature, at any rate, stands out; for behind all the activities there lies the intention to bring about learning. It is not that teaching, in most of its uses, implies that anybody necessarily learns anything. Rather it implies that the teacher intends to bring about learning.

To begin by seeing teaching as consisting simply of activities with this intention, whatever particular form they might take, can be important in liberating us from a restricted view that confines teaching to such traditional methods as instructing and demonstrating. As was pointed out earlier, the kinds of things we want pupils to learn are immensely varied in character – concepts, beliefs, skills, habits, attitudes, etc. The processes of learning were seen to be equally varied. It is, therefore, not surprising that the activities of trying to bring about such varied forms of learning are in their turn equally diverse. Again, if at some point the learning we want is best achieved by pupils being given opportunity to determine their own sequence of activities, or to discover things for themselves, then to organize for these may be part, if not the whole, of one's teaching. For if teaching has no other point or intention than learning, such planning would seem to fall well within the meaning of the term.

Yet stressing learning activities at the expense of a grasp of the correlative teaching activities that are necessarily part of schooling, can distort the enterprise. Enquiry, discovery, research, trial and error, are all, for instance, forms of learning. But their natural home would seem to be in contexts where the person is learning essentially on his own, where as a matter of fact there is no teacher, or where there could not possibly be a teacher, because what is to be learnt is as yet unknown. These activities are precisely those by which one learns without being taught. But, by contrast, the whole point of schooling is that there is a teacher whose function it is to bring about learning in the best possible way. In this context elements of enquiry, discovery, research and trial and error, may all have a part, but these cannot, by the nature of the case, together constitute schooling. And, employed within schooling, they are deliberately used in a controlled context, within which they are at least believed to be the best way of reaching certain specifiable objectives. They are here as much part of a deliberately planned scheme of teaching, as activities of instruction and demonstration might be. It is not that schooling limits the kind of learning activities that are permissible; it is rather that within schooling the activities necessarily become part of intentional planning, which starts with deciding the specific objectives of the enterprise, and which goes on to organize the best means of achieving these. Granted this context, it must be remembered that there is, in general, no reason to suppose that the way things were originally discovered, is the best way for pupils to learn them once they are known. It is perhaps worth adding here that nothing that has been said must be taken to imply that pupils shall have no choice in the learning activities in which they will be involved. As in the case of curricular objectives and curriculum organization, the point is that ultimately the decision, in all these cases, must rest necessarily in other hands, namely those of the teacher. The issue is invariably one for his judgment: 'What are the best learning activities, given specified objectives?' Too often the debate over the best activities becomes deflected and confused because the objectives have not been agreed in the first instance.

c *Indicating what is to be learnt*   But can we say anything further about teaching activities, beyond the fact that their intention is that of bringing about learning? Certainly two things can be said that, not surprisingly, relate to the two features that would seem to characterize learning. As it was pointed out earlier, it is always, necessarily, the case that some particular thing is being learnt, and equally the case that the process involves, in some sense, the experience of the particular learner. Where teaching is concerned, it is likewise the case that something is necessarily being taught to someone. Taking the first of these considerations, it would be distinctly odd to claim that one was teaching something if one's activities did not, by some means or other, present precisely what one intends to be learnt. However firm one's intention to teach swimming might be, it would be absurd to count an analysis of English grammatical structure, or even a presentation of how to solve certain equations in hydrodynamics, as in fact teaching swimming. Clearly it is necessary for one's intentions to take effect in activities which, if not overtly, at least by implication, exhibit, display, express or explain to the learner, what is to be learnt. Skill in the many forms of presenting the diverse elements to be learnt, be it in instruction, designing work cards, performing demonstrations or organizing the environment for discovery, is essential to teaching. Yet it is instructive to note that many, if not all, such forms of presentation, are important in other contexts –

particularly in entertainment. In teaching, what is distinctive is the intention in the presentation that the pupils shall achieve some form of mastery which they did not previously possess, an intention not to be confused with the achieving of enjoyment or laughter.

This necessity for teaching activities to indicate or express some content, that pupils are intended to learn, serves to distinguish clearly those activities which are essentially teaching, from many which are not, however valuable they may be in the circumstances. In teaching French, for instance, parts of the language must in some way be presented to pupils so that they can hear it spoken, see it written and so on. To compliment, smile at or reward pupils, who are successful, is no more an intrinsic part of teaching French than keeping the room at a comfortable temperature. Conditions of this sort might, as a matter of empirical fact, facilitate the pupils' learning, thus functioning as extrinsic aids. But they are neither part of what we mean by 'learning', nor part of what we mean by 'teaching', at least in any specific sense. There is, of course, a more general use of the term 'teaching', which covers not only specifically teaching activities, but also those which as a matter of contingent fact do aid the process. In practice, the latter are immensely important, yet it is vital to a proper understanding of what teaching is, that they are not confused with those activities necessary for any teaching to be going on at all. Ideal conditions and extrinsic motivation are neither necessary nor sufficient for either teaching or learning, however valuable they may prove as aids to them.

d *The learner's cognitive state*   But, granted all that has been said, we might still have difficulty in describing as 'teaching' some activities which express most clearly what it is intended that pupils should learn. For such activities may show no appreciation whatever of what the pupils can, as a matter of fact, learn. Could the reading of a poem in Russian to a group of pupils, who had no knowledge of that language, be teaching them the appreciation of the poem? Or would a lecture on the differential calculus, designed for undergraduates, be considered teaching, if presented to a class of average ten-year-olds? Surely the trouble, in these cases, is that the activities have been conducted without any concern for the simple logical point that all teaching is, at least in principle, teaching somebody, as well as teaching something. And just as a specific activity must necessarily indicate the particular something being taught, so it must also necessarily indicate this in a way intelligible to the particular pupils concerned. It may seem a very strong demand to insist that failure to appreciate what pupils can learn puts the activity altogether outside the category of 'teaching'. Certainly in using the term we rarely pay explicit attention to this point. Yet in any context the matter has to be considered and it is to the credit of advocates of the more 'progressive' approach to teaching, as we argued in Chs. 2 and 3, that they have made the point explicitly, insisting so forcefully on the necessity for teachers working from the existing cognitive state of their pupils. More 'traditional' approaches have tended to think explicitly only about clearly expressing what is to be learnt, taking a knowledge of the pupils' cognitive state for granted. If this analysis is correct, however, 'teaching' necessitates explicit attention to both aspects, and it is in terms of this attention that good teaching can be distinguished from bad.

It was noted earlier that in contemporary use of the term 'learning', different demands are at times made on the kind of activity or process which is being picked out. Sometimes the term is restricted to non-causal, conscious processes; at other times unconscious, or even, in very extended uses, causal processes are admitted. If we are not implicitly to legislate a meaning of 'teaching', a similar variety of contemporary usage must here be recognized. Three logically necessary conditions for the central cases of 'teaching' activities have been suggested: (i) they must be conducted with the intention of bringing about learning, (ii) they must indicate or exhibit what is to be learnt, (iii) they must do this in a way which is intelligible to, and within the capacities of, the learners. It is thus possible that there are cases of 'teaching' that disregard any one or even two of these conditions, and yet are understood derivatively as cases of 'teaching'. Weakening the force of each of the last two conditions has been commented on in previous paragraphs. Weakening the force of the first is however worth noting, as the activities then characterized do at times seem to be important in education. Manifestly it is not infrequently the case that a person's activities, the intention of which has nothing to do with the bringing about of learning, are the means whereby someone learns. In such circumstances the former may be said to have taught the latter. Observing someone performing a particular physical skill, or solving a difficult mathematical problem, might 'teach' a person a great deal. The use of the term 'teaching' in such cases has at least this justification, that even if it was not intended, the activity, as a matter of fact, expressed something the observer had not already mastered, and it was possible for him, because of his cognitive state, to learn it on this occasion. It may well be that much of our learning occurs in this way. Indeed in some cases, particularly in the arts and social learning, there may be little else we can do about teaching beyond having certain activities going on in the school community. Yet, clearly, to plan deliberately for such activities, so that others will learn, is to take a first step towards teaching in a fully intentional sense. By definition such teaching occurs just as soon as the activity itself is influenced by any consideration of the would-be learners.

e *Content and methods*   In all that has been said we have been at pains to maintain a balance of emphasis between, on the one hand, the vast range of specific activities that can constitute teaching, and on the other, the important necessary conditions that must be satisfied. The choice of the best specific activities in any given case depends on many particular factors that are not of a philosophical nature. However, two further philosophical considerations, that arise when the planning of specific activities is being considered, are worthy of mention. First, it is important to distinguish (a) what is to be learnt as a result of the teaching-learning activities that are being planned, (b) the content or subject matter to be used to express what is to be learnt, and (c) the method or form of presentation of this content. Concern for the first of these brings to the fore yet again the need to be clear about the objectives being pursued. The other two indicate separable, if related, aspects of the means to these objectives. Granted certain objectives to be reached by learning, it is in many cases possible to indicate or express these by means of a number of alternative forms of content. Particularly is this true in teaching an understanding of such abstract notions as, say, democracy or classical symphonic form, where the particular expressions of these can be very varied. What is more, granted a particular content, the precise method of presentation can be varied too. Granted that the approach to democracy is to use, as content, contemporary British political procedures, rather than the historical development of the concept from early Greek notions, is the method of presentation to be one in which these procedures are described analytically, observed directly in action, simulated in the school, or illustrated in film? Or is the Mozart symphony, selected for the content, to be analysed by pupils individually after hearing it at a concert, to be got at from the score, to be analysed by the teacher in a blackboard summary, or to be elucidated in a 'hunt the theme' musical quiz?

Yet, as was pointed out in Ch. 4, such a means-ends picture of the practical planning of education, distorts the situation if it is interpreted in a crude instrumental way. The content and method used are not related to the objectives in a purely *de facto* manner, if only because the content and method themselves express and embody objectives. The content itself is being mastered and, if primarily for the sake of some other objective, such mastery is in general to be thought of as an objective in its own right. Methods likewise have this double significance, involving in themselves the exercise of skills of immediate educational value. These considerations do, of course, limit to some extent the content and methods which carefully planned education employs. Yet, in the interests of finding more effective teaching methods than those which have been most common in the past, it must be recognized that, in general, the choice of objectives leaves undetermined both the precise content and the precise methods to be used. That the specific content and formal methods, used in traditional grammar school education, have proved ineffective with less able children provides no justification for rejecting the aims of that education for the less able. Nor is the only alternative that of 'taking the work more slowly'. What is needed, if the objectives are indeed valuable for all, is a radical reconsideration of the content and method used under these conditions.

The second point, that comes to the fore at this level of planning, is the extent to which the complex interrelation of objectives does in fact determine a teaching sequence. The argument, that each of the modes of objective experience and knowledge outlined earlier has a distinctive inherent logical structure, is sometimes taken to mean that there is a strictly necessary temporal sequence to the order in which its central concepts and propositions can be learnt. If so, this would determine an order in which they must be taught. Such a view commits a similar mistake to that of curriculum planners, who see the logical distinctions between different modes of experience as necessarily implying an organization of the curriculum into separate subjects. But, once again, a pattern of ends or achievements must not be confused with a pattern of means. In the mastery of concepts and propositions it is not true, except in very particular cases, that the logical interrelations between these elements mark out an order of hierarchical interdependence that governs their intelligibility. Only if that were the case would there be a unique sequence for teaching and learning. Understanding and knowledge, however, are not in general built brick on brick, according to a hierarchical pattern. For the most part, our grasp of the meanings of terms, and of the justification of claims, comes with the establishing of interconnected concepts and truths whose links may be forged in a diversity of orders, just as they may be forged with a diversity of content and methods. That this is not the whole story is borne out by the sequences mentioned earlier, which Kohlberg, Piaget and others claim to have discovered in the acquisition of categoreal concepts and principles. The sequences here would certainly seem to reflect, at times, certain logical priorities that do determine intelligibility. Detailed conclusions on the point are, however, difficult to establish. All that can be said, at present, is that the precise restrictions on teaching and learning need to be examined in individual, particular cases. The idea that there is behind all learning, if we analyse its sequence closely enough, one and only one sequence, is surely another myth that has improperly restricted our approaches to teaching for far too long.

3 The specific activities of teaching and learning

In discussing teaching and learning no attention has been paid to the more specific forms which these might take, and for a consideration of these readers must be referred elsewhere. The foregoing general discussion will, it is hoped, have provided a framework within which some preliminary characterization of these is possible. Using the principle distinctions made already, activities within the broadest band of learning might be distinguished according to the particular types of mastery, or the particular types of experience, or the causal processes involved. That some forms of learning are, at least in part, picked out by the absence of teaching, has already been commented on. Similarly, where teaching is concerned, distinctions in its activities can be made by looking at the types of objectives, content, or methods involved. In a more shorthand way, types of teaching can be distinguished by reference to the types of learning at which it aims. Clarification of what exactly is meant, for instance, by 'instruction' and 'training', would serve to elucidate in what specific contexts it is proper to employ these terms and on what factors precisely the use of them turns. Loose application of such words, when the necessary conditions for them are not fulfilled, can mislead unwary teachers into quite inadequate forms of activity whose outcome cannot possibly be what they intend. It has been fondly hoped by some that certain activities, labelled 'play' and 'enquiry', would lead to learning, when elements necessary to the situation, if learning was to be possible, have been missing. The immensely varied use of the fashionable term 'socialization', sometimes picking out certain objectives, sometimes certain learning procedures, sometimes thought of as a form of teaching, sometimes contrasted with teaching, illustrates only too well the degree of confusion within much debate on educational processes. The precise analysis of what is meant by such terms within the teaching context is of major importance, and is already bearing valuable fruit.

4 Teaching, learning and education

Much of this chapter has been concerned with the activities of teaching and learning in general, rather than the forms they take in the particular context of education. In conclusion, then, we must ask if education, in our specific sense, places any restriction on the wide range of activities that fall under these labels. If education is taken to centre on developing desirable states of mind involving knowledge and understanding, it must be clearly understood that this involves specific objectives of a vast variety, stretching right across Bloom's cognitive, affective and psycho-motor domains. It in no sense excludes, for instance, the development of physical skills, though these must necessarily be seen in relation to the person's development of understanding and other mental characteristics that can give a proper significance and place to such skills in his life. Education, in this sense, will therefore grant a limited place to activities like drill in specific physical movements, because of their very limited achievements. It will not exclude them. Bearing this in mind, the variety of the objectives included in education means that almost every possible type of learning and teaching can have some place in the over-all enterprise.

What will be excluded, however, are those activities which are necessarily inconsistent with the 'value' and 'knowledge' criteria which the concept of 'education' involves (see Ch. 2). In terms of the 'knowledge' criterion education would seem to exclude all those peripheral processes of teaching and learning which deliberately seek to achieve forms of unthinking behavioural response. In so far as they deliberately seek to exclude the possibility of the person understanding what he is doing, critically assessing it, and perhaps changing his behaviour, these activities would seem to directly contradict the knowledge criterion. Such forms of behaviour may, from other points of view, have value and indeed may at times be necessary in the interests of mere physical survival. Yet they cannot be regarded as educational achievements. Of more interest, because more controversial, however, are those obviously central teaching and learning processes which do intentionally promote thought, criticism and considered action, but deliberately seek for some purpose to restrict the cognitive framework within which these occur. Though what is achieved may have other values, and such processes may even develop, incidentally, something of limited educational value, the major aim must again be rejected as incompatible with the knowledge criterion. To prevent understanding and knowledge at any point must necessarily be anti-educational. It is for this reason that much that falls under that elusive term 'indoctrination' must be excluded. Those activities, that do not seek to prevent the achievement of understanding, but merely do not encourage it, have a somewhat ambiguous status. If not to be regarded as of negative educational value, they can hardly be looked on with much positive favour. The activities just commented on have been taken to be fully intentional and deliberate on the part of the teacher. Yet should the ends that characterize them be achieved without any such intentions, from an educational point of view they must still be rejected. For this reason alone, a thorough empirical investigation of the consequences of teaching activities needs to be undertaken, that goes beyond those consequences intended by the teachers. Only in this way can we hope to control miseducation that results from the very best of educational intentions.

The 'value' criterion of education, being more general than the 'knowledge' criterion, has more limited, if not less important, significance. The complex interconnection between means and ends, that has been commented on more than once, implies that the processes of education must not be assessed in simple utilitarian terms. If the content and methods of education are themselves being mastered as subsidiary objectives, they should, like the more immediate objectives, be judged on educational grounds. Learning to learn and learning by enquiry have indeed become prominent explicit curriculum objectives of late, a change giving added point to the importance of what are only too often regarded as merely the instrumental aspects of education. Educational activities must therefore themselves be assessed in educational terms, not simply in those of utilitarian efficiency as serving other ends. In practice such assessment is difficult, partly because of our ignorance of the empirical facts about different teaching and learning activities. It is made yet more difficult owing to our lack of agreement on those things we do indeed consider educationally valuable. Once more our elucidation has brought us up against the crucial place of value judgments in education, judgments which clearly must govern not only the ends or aims of education but the processes of teaching and learning as well. At present our educational values do little to rule out many possible forms of teaching and learning. Those that are excluded are usually rejected on the yet wider grounds of general moral unacceptability.

We conclude, then, that educational processes are those processes of learning, which may be stimulated by teaching, out of which desirable states of mind, involving knowledge and understanding, develop. There are many such processes – learning by experience, from example, from personal instruction, from teaching machines, and so on. In recent times the discussion of these processes has tended to polarize into those favouring a 'traditional' teacher-centred approach and those favouring a 'progressive' pupil-centred approach. It is our belief that both these 'models' are one-sided. A fuller analysis suggests that the processes of education are more complex than either side suggests, and that a doctrinaire insistence on any limited range of activities can only be unprofitably restrictive.

6

Teaching and personal relationships

Introduction

It was argued in Ch. 2 that, though the progressive movement in education has often suffered from indeterminacy with regard to aims and content, it has certainly exhibited moral and psychological enlightenment with regard to method. The epithet 'child-centred' indicates the general focus of this enlightenment. Teachers, it is argued, should not regard their pupils just as potential recipients of knowledge and skill; they should enter into personal relationships with them. The class-room should not be like a parade ground in which generation after generation of reluctant recruits are licked into shape; rather it should be permeated by a happy atmosphere which is the by-product of good personal relationships. At the university level, too, the teacher should not be completely wrapped up in his own research, interesting himself only in those students who can help him with it. He should emerge from his ivory tower and have more time for students as persons. Education is not just a matter of the meeting of minds; it is a process of personal encounter.

Such exhortations seem peculiarly pertinent at the present time when educational institutions are constantly expanding and when economic pressures are beginning to dictate an increase in the staff-student ratio. Mammoth-sized classes are increasingly assembled before which the professor, like a performer on television, has to display his wares in as arresting a manner as possible. This makes discussion of his views with his pupils and personal contact with them very difficult to contrive. Schools, too, become so large that it is impossible for a teacher to get to know his pupils; so guidance officers or counsellors are introduced to provide some kind of personal attention in a thoroughly depersonalized situation. The teacher becomes just a lecturer in a subject and is perceived by the pupils as being purely a purveyor of knowledge which is necessary for mounting the ladder of the occupational structure.

For educational institutions to be successful some kind of intrinsic motivation is essential, an identification on the part of the pupils with the educational purposes of such institutions. But their size and depersonalization militates against this. Instead of teachers providing a link between the generations, and thus facilitating the transmission of these purposes, they tend to be regarded as part of an impersonal order from which the pupils remain alienated, huddled together, perhaps, in their own peer-group culture.

In this type of situation what is to be made of the suggestion that teachers should try to develop personal relationships with pupils? Is it compatible with their role as teachers concerned with the development of knowledge and understanding? And how *can* a teacher develop personal relationships with a class of over forty? Is a personal relationship possible with a child of ten? Is not such talk impractical sentimentality? These are reasonable questions, but no answer can be given to them until there is more clarity about what we mean by 'personal relationships' and how they are distinct from or related to the role relationship between teacher and pupil. Let us, therefore, approach these problems by trying to distinguish various relations in which the teacher stands to pupils. The hope is that we shall eventually be able to isolate what is meant by 'personal relationships'. In this process of analysis the reader may sense at times some affront to his unreflective assumptions about personal relationships. He may, indeed, say at the end 'But that's not what I mean by "personal relationships".' But the term is a very vague one in ordinary use and, provided that the analysis sharpens up distinctions which are relevant for understanding and decision-making, such affronts must be risked. For, as we have stressed before, the purpose of conceptual analysis is not to reveal some essence which ordinary language reflects, but to get clearer about how things are and about what is to be done

1 Teaching and respect for persons

In any institution people occupy positions which require them to act in various ways which are demanded by their role. A teacher is expected to treat a pupil in a certain way as a learner, just as a bus-conductor is expected to treat an individual in a certain way as a passenger. In other words, whatever else a teacher is expected to do, at least he is expected to teach.

a *Requirements implicit in teaching* Teaching, as an activity, is unintelligible unless somebody is or is thought of as a learner. The view which a teacher has of his pupils as learners should, therefore, provide a thread of unity which runs through a whole range of his dealings with them – varying from conversations with them about their visit to the cinema to having to punish them in order to safeguard the conditions necessary for learning to proceed. It also dictates a certain degree of interest in pupils as individuals; for as teaching necessarily involves marking out, explaining, and putting individuals in the way of a whole variety of things to be learnt, the teacher must have regard to the stages at which individuals are if he is to teach and not simply loose off ideas in the presence of his pupils. In other words attention must be paid to the conceptual structure and motivation of pupils so that some kind of match can be managed between what they have already mastered and what they have yet to master. There need not, however, be anything particularly 'personal' about this role-relationship. For pupils can be dealt with in a very 'impersonal' way. A circus-trainer, who teaches animals a variety of complicated tricks, presumably has a similar attitude to his charges in so far as he too regards them as learners.

b *Moral principles – especially respect for persons* Teachers, however, are usually concerned with education and this places additional restrictions and requirements on their teaching. They are expected to teach what is valuable as distinct from trivial things like Bingo or wicked things like burglary and fraud. They are also expected both to conform to and to pass on certain moral standards in dealing with their pupils. Of particular importance are wide-ranging moral principles, which are not confined to their role, such as benevolence, fairness and freedom. These principles are, of course, made concrete and modified in their application by the special relationship in which a teacher stands to his pupils. Benevolence, for instance, or the consideration of interests, is partly made concrete in a special relationship in so far as a teacher stands *in loco parentis*; the principle of freedom has to be modified in its application because the wants of children are as yet indeterminate and because all sorts of constraints are necessary in order that children can learn. But the reason for such principles is not grounded purely in the teacher's role and their sphere of application extends far beyond his role. A teacher should be concerned, for instance, about a boy breaking his arm irrespective of whether this hinders or helps him as a learner.

Amongst such far-ranging moral principles is that of respect for persons. As this principle may overlap with having a personal relationship with someone it requires rather more detailed treatment in the context of this chapter than other moral principles which criss-cross the institutional role of the teacher.

It is important, first of all, to distinguish the rather abstract principle of respect for persons from the use of 'respect' in more concrete contexts in which respect is shown in so far as someone occupies a certain position or excels at some activity. If we say, for instance, that a man is no respecter of persons we sometimes mean that he does not show the deference thought to be due to another who occupies a superior position in an hierarchy. Perhaps he does not rise from his chair when his headmaster enters the staff-room; perhaps he is as prepared to tell the headmaster what he thinks of his behaviour to his secretary as he is prepared to tell the secretary what he thinks of her behaviour towards the head-master. Alternatively we talk about someone having a healthy respect for someone else in so far as he recognizes that he is good at something. A boxer may have a healthy respect for an opponent who can deliver a vicious right hook; a politician may have a similar sort of respect for another who can make telling points in debate.

In some cases such respect, which is connected with specific positions or achievements, unfortunately becomes generalized. People are thought to be *generally* superior or inferior as human beings and a more generalized attitude of respect or contempt is developed towards them. One of the unfortunate consequences, for instance, of the 11-plus selective examination in England was that those who failed were often thought to be, and thought of them-selves as being, not just worse *at* certain intellectual performances but inferior generally as human beings. When they are treated as such we say that lack of respect is being shown to them as persons, as human beings deserving to be treated with dignity as becomes any human being. When this sort of thing is said the more abstract concept of respect for persons, which is the fundamental moral principle with which we are here concerned, is being applied.

To feel respect for persons in this more abstract sense is to be moved by the thought that another is, after all, a person like one-self and that, as such, he is to be accorded certain rights and to be treated with consideration. What, then, corresponds, in this more abstract case, to the view of someone as superior in an hier-archy or good at a performance, which goes with the more con-crete applications of respect? It is not, surely, just the thought that someone is alive, is capable of feeling pain, and is a centre of wants and expectations. For we can, without impropriety, ascribe all such modes of consciousness to rabbits or rats; and we would not speak of respecting them as persons. Surely by speaking of individuals as persons we draw attention to a group of more typi-cally human characteristics that animals do not share with human beings, which are connected with having an assertive point of view. We think of individuals as being capable of valuation and choice, of formulating intentions and making decisions which, to a certain extent, determine their destiny; we think of them as taking pride in their achievements and of being conscience-stricken about their short-comings. Animals do not have a point of view in this articulated sense. In so far as we think of an individual as having a point of view, and in so far as this is not a matter of indifference to us, we respect him as a person. To show lack of respect for persons, is, for instance, to ignore his point of view when we use him purely for our own purposes or to settle his destiny for him without taking account of his views about it, or to treat him purely as the occupant of a role by ignoring his more general status as a rational being.

How does respect for persons so understood enter into the teaching situation? How is this general attitude towards another as a human being related to a teacher's more specific attitude to him as a learner? Obviously more is required than the minimum of understanding of and interest in an individual as a learner which is necessary to match what is being taught to his conceptual and motivational structure; for he must not be regarded merely in his role as a learner. His view of himself as a learner, his aspirations and pride in his achievements, however puny, are things about him as a human being that matter to anyone who has respect for persons. He must not be thought of just as subject-fodder or as a potential performer who can be equipped with a repertoire of skills.

On the other hand a teacher is a teacher as well as a rational being. As such he must have regard also to the values immanent in what he is teaching. He must not be so overwhelmed with awe at the thought of another expressing his innermost thoughts that he omits to point out that they are not very clearly expressed or scarcely relevant to the matter under discussion. An art teacher who is content to let children express themselves, without any concern for aesthetic standards, is deficient as a teacher whatever his or her merits as a respecter of persons. In practice those teachers who have regard to the standards of their subject, and who also have respect for persons, work with due regard to both types of value by envisaging a standard relative to the individual pupil. They are mindful both of the point of view of the pupil and of the objective standards immanent in the skill or form of experience that they are trying to pass on. They require that pupils shall 'do their best'. The concept of 'doing one's best' takes account of the standards of the skill or mode of experience in question, of the ability and stage of development of the learner and of his point of view as a human being.

Now many might argue that a teacher, in so far as he is teaching and not just lecturing, must be having personal relationships with his pupils; for he must have regard to the motivation and conceptual structure of learners, which are personal attributes. In so far, too, as he respects them as persons, he is having regard to other general personal qualities. So any teacher, who is *teaching* in a morally acceptable manner, must, by definition, be having personal relationships with pupils. Such relationships are required by his role as a teacher. This can, of course, be said. But it is a way of using the term 'personal relationship' which ignores important distinctions that many would insist on making. For many teachers, who satisfy all such role and moral requirements, would nevertheless deny that they are having personal relationships with their pupils. Personal relationships, they might say, are the sorts of relationships which they enjoy with their friends and with their wives. Their relationships with their pupils are very different. What, then, are they talking about when they talk about 'personal relationships'? Whether or not their way of talking is universal is of minor importance. What matters, philosophically speaking, is to get clearer about the features of the relationships which they refer to in this way.

2   What are personal relationships?

Let us first of all make a somewhat arbitrary distinction between personal relations and personal relationships. If questions are asked about a teacher's personal relations with his pupils information is usually required about whether he is friendly, cruel or kind to them and whether they like him or dislike him, trust him or distrust him, envy him or admire him and so on. Attention is being drawn to his attitudes to his pupils and to their reactions to him as distinct from his knowledge of his subject, his articulateness in exposition, his efficiency in class-management, and so on.

Ordinary usage is not decisive on the use of the word 'relationship' instead of 'relation'; but the general tendency is to use 'relationship' when something more structured and reciprocal is being picked out. We might describe a salesman as having good personal relations with his customers; but it would seem a bit extravagant to describe him as having good personal relationships with them. That would suggest more the style of the grocer in the village shop than of the salesman in the multiple store. The politician who charms his audience on television may be admired or hated by innumerable individuals, but he need not enter into a personal relationship with any of them. 'Relationship' suggests something more structured that grows up between or is entered into by the people concerned, and in which there is some element of reciprocity. This arises not from some impersonal order, whether of role, of convention or of morality, but from the initiative of the individuals concerned.

a *The content of personal relationships* How, then, are personal relationships to be characterized? It might be thought that there is some distinctive content to them. One of their most obvious features, so it might be thought, is that they involve reciprocal knowledge of private matters, as distinct from matters connected with the public institutionalized contexts in which people may encounter each other. By this is meant some knowledge both of the details of the private lives of the people concerned and of their motives, attitudes and aspirations. In a fully developed personal relationship people reveal such things to each other and, to a certain extent, they build up a common world which they share together. This is constituted not simply by their shared experiences but also by the common stock of knowledge which has developed as a result of being kept informed about a whole variety of private matters. When they meet they keep each other up to date, as it were, about the details of the private worlds that intersect on such occasions.

This, however, is characteristic of what might be called a fully developed personal relationship. There are other cases, in which we would say that people enter into a personal relationship with each other, where there is nothing like this degree of mutual disclosure. Suppose that A and B, who hardly know each other, are at a committee meeting, and suppose that A, in the middle of a boring discussion, starts perusing his *Good Food Guide* in search of a restaurant. He looks up guiltily and is aware of a knowing look from B who passes him a note. In the note is written the name of a restaurant near at hand. A acknowledges the message with a grateful nod. Surely this would be regarded as an embryonic sort of personal relationship even though A and B never see each other again, and therefore are unable to build up anything further between them.

Conversely there can be situations in which a great deal of private information is revealed by individuals in which we would not say that a personal relationship is being built up or enjoyed; for something must also be added about the aspect under which this sort of knowledge is sought or disclosed. Otherwise we would not be able to distinguish a personal relationship from the sharing of private knowledge in the context of institutions and semi-formalized activities. In a literature class, for instance, those participating in the discussion of a poem or novel, may contribute their private experience to a common pool in order to arrive at a better understanding of the author's meaning. But they would not be described as entering into a personal relationship on that account. A teacher, too, might reminisce about his own private life in order to illustrate a point, or probe into the details of a pupil's home background in order to teach him better. But as the personal details would be disclosed or elicited under the aspect of treating another as a learner, we would not describe the teacher as entering into a personal relationship with the pupil, in the sense of 'personal relationship' which we are exploring.

What these cases bring out is, firstly, that something must be reciprocated, as in the committee case, but personal knowledge would seem too rich a notion to cover such cases of embryonic personal relationships; secondly and more important, that it is not so much the content that matters, in characterizing a personal relationship, as the aspect under which the content is viewed. For it was the aspect under which personal knowledge was disclosed or sought that ruled out the teaching of literature case as an example of entering into a personal relationship.

b *Under what aspect?* How, then, are we to pick out the aspect under which such disclosures must be viewed before we can properly talk of personal relationships? Can we only negatively say that they must not be cases where the exchange takes place in the context of an institutionalized relationship or of some activity which puts the stamp of some extraneous purpose upon it? Can nothing more positive be said?

It might be suggested that some kind of liking or attraction between the persons concerned is what must be present to convert such disclosures into a personal relationship. But this surely is not even empirically necessary for a personal relationship to develop, let alone part of our understanding of what a personal relationship is. Two women might meet on the top of a bus, and before long, they might be swapping all sorts of details about their confinements, maladies, hopes and regrets. But they might have been led to do this, not by any mutual liking or attraction, but by an announcement on a placard about Sophia Loren's baby. Would we not say that they had entered into a personal relationship – especially if they met again a week later on the same bus and continued their conversation at the point where they had left off – without asking any further questions about whether they liked each other or not? Liking, of course, is a frequent *occasion* for the development of personal relationships in that it predisposes people to enter into them. But it does not seem to be necessary to them.

It might be argued that respect for another is the attitude under which we view him which is distinctive of entering into a personal relationship. For, after all, is not 'respect' the appropriate attitude to have for a person? It is indeed in so far as we are treating him morally. But respect for persons can be interpreted only as a negative counsel prohibiting the use of another as a means to one's own ends or treating him just as a functionary. Respect for persons need not issue in any positive outgoingness which requires any kind of reciprocal response. Also a very intimate personal relationship may be enjoyed in which respect for persons is lacking. Sexual attraction, for instance, may lead to a great deal of personal knowledge on both sides; but one party may be using the other for his own sexual ends without much respect for the other as a person. Maybe we would say that such a personal relationship, in which there is lack of respect for persons, is a bad personal relationship; but it remains nevertheless a personal relationship.

Respect, then, is altogether too disinterested and rational to pick out the required aspect. It is too much connected with thinking of another as having rights. Is not sympathy, therefore, more on the right lines; for it suggests a more outgoing type of attitude which is connected with responses at a level below that of morality, custom, and institutionalized roles? When we feel sympathy we do not necessarily feel attracted by another either, as in liking, any more than we are moved by the thought of another as a moral being. We are receptive to him at an affective level – as someone, like ourselves, who has desires, wishes and inclinations, who is sensitive to pain, and various other passive states. Sympathy, however, will not quite do; for it seems associated with seeing another only as a sufferer. We do not usually talk of sympathy when we are responsive to the joy or pleasure of another; yet often in personal relationships this is very much to the fore. It also carries a slight suggestion of the involuntary, whereas in personal relationships we seem much more to commit ourselves voluntarily to another and to require some kind of response.

The nearest we can get to characterizing the positive attitude under which we view another, with whom we enter into a personal relationship, is brought out by words such as 'interest in' and 'concern for' another as a human being, together with some kind of openness or giving on one's own part. This must be a response to another *simply* as a human being, who is subject to pleasure and pain and the usual gamut of emotions and desires. In other words this attitude to another must not be connected with any extraneous purpose, whether individual or shared. He must not be thought of as a means to one's ends or just as a co-operator or competitor in a common pursuit. Neither need it involve moralization as in concern for his good or in respect for him as a subject of rights and the determiner of his own destiny. It is simply a receptiveness to him and an outgoingness towards him as an individual human being. In institutionalized situations, when personal relationships are entered into, as in the case of the committee, B must sense that A is, to a certain extent, stepping outside his role and responding to him as an individual, and vice versa. Such interest is not particularized enough or strong enough to count as liking. It differs from respect in that it does not fasten on the possibility of a person's rights or dignity as a chooser being infringed. It is difficult to pin it down in positive terms; but without some such attitude there is no way of distinguishing passing the time of day with someone from entering into a personal relationship with him. What *is* the difference between saying 'How do you do?' to someone as a matter of manners, and entering into a serious discussion about his health?

Personal relationships can be very one-sided. A may be very shy and inarticulate about his own life and worries and B may be very articulate and embarrassingly open about his private life, but so egocentric or overwhelmed by his own predicament that he is singularly insensitive to that of others. When A and B meet, B with A's encouragement, may do most of the disclosing, with the result that A's private life remains more or less a closed book to B. But even in this one-sided type of relationship there is still an element of reciprocity. There is on A's part, as well as his concern for B, some openness or giving, even though this does not take the form of being articulate or informative about his own life. He conveys, by his glances, promptings, and encouragement, that he cares. And this is to venture something about himself which many cannot.

What seems to emerge from this analysis is that the constituent of personal disclosure, with which we started, can be of a very minimal sort. In elucidating what is meant by a 'personal relationship' the aspect under which a person is viewed is of central importance. It has been difficult to characterize this aspect save in negative terms such as not required by a role, by morals, or by a common interest or extraneous purpose. But some attempt has been made to do this in terms of an interest in and reaction to another as a human being. Receiving another's confidences and self-disclosure are prominent in personal relationships because these are the most explicit and palpable ways in which such an interest or concern is manifest.

We are, of course, protected against the risks and embarrassments of personal relationships during much of our waking lives. Our institutional roles require certain forms of response to others from us; manners, too, create fences between us and our neighbours on which we can lean and converse with them about mundane matters without revealing much of ourselves. Common interests unite us and turn our interests outwards towards shared goals and ideals rather than into the recesses of each other's hearts; and, as moral beings, we confront each other on a disinterested, rule-governed plane. Personal relationships only begin when we respond to a glimpse of what lies behind these façades, and when something slips from under our own. In certain cases and with certain people all that may slip out is an interest in or concern for another that is not demanded by a role and which exceeds what is morally required of us.

There is, of course, a kind of vulnerability which is endemic to personal relationships. By revealing too much of ourselves we may put ourselves at the mercy of others who may later become antagonistic to us; by exhibiting an openness to another we also risk rebuff. Unscrupulous people, too, may go through the motions of entering into personal relationships for their own ends, and most of us are only too prone to self-deceit or *mauvaise foi* in deluding ourselves about our motives in such matters.

Ideally such responses are reciprocated in a full sense and develop into mutual trust, commitment, and loyalty, as is found in friendship and marriage. Our personal relationships are thus like a series of concentric rings. On the outer edge are those with whom we have only fleeting encounters of this sort where there is a modicum of interest but little in the way of a developed reciprocal relationship; in the inner circle are perhaps one or two with whom we may share all that is most intimate about our private lives, motives, and aspirations. What has emerged as a personal relationship may seem much more mundane than the I-Thou confrontation that is sometimes held up as an ideal. But to be near the earth is not altogether unbecoming for those who live on it.

3 Personal relationships in teaching

In order to explore what might be meant by developing personal relationships with pupils we first of all got out of the way relations with which we are contrasting such personal relationships, namely those involved in the role relationship of teacher to pupil in so far as he treats a pupil as a learner, and more general moral relationships relevant to the teaching situation, especially that of respect for persons. This left us with the more individualized and more affective relations and relationships in which the teacher might stand to his pupils as one human being to another. Within this general area it will be convenient to distinguish three levels which seem to be implicit in our analysis. There is, first of all, the general substrate of a teacher's *relations* with his pupils in so far as this is permeated by likes and dislikes, loves and hates, and other such generalized attractions and aversions. There is, secondly, the possibility and desirability of his having what might be called *fully developed* personal relationships with his pupils. There is, thirdly, the possibility and desirability of his having what might be called *embryonic* personal relationships with them.

a *Personal relations*   About a teacher's personal relations, in this very generalized affective sense, there is not a great deal to be said. For as the teacher is an individual human being as well as an occupant of a role and a moral agent subject to impersonal public principles, he is bound to be subject to a whole gamut of individualized reactions. As an individual human being dealing with other individual human beings he is bound to react somewhat differently to them. He may like or dislike some of them. Such reactions, however, are not laid down by his role. There is no requirement, for instance, that he should like or love all of them – in so far as love denotes an a-rational attraction and is distinct from respecting them as persons. Such attractions are particularized and cannot be commanded. They form part of the emotional and motivational substrate on which the teacher has to erect consistent forms of conduct. To be widely influenced by them would obviously be inconsistent with fairness and with the role relationship in which he stands to every pupil. No doubt if a teacher is of a friendly disposition and finds the constant company of children congenial to him he is more likely to be successful than if they irritate and bore him to death. But there are limits to what he can do about this; for children are very quick to sense certain forms of insincerity. Similarly whether he is liked or disliked is a very chancy and idiosyncratic matter, and again, this is not something that he can immediately do much about. He cannot, as it were, polish up his charisma in front of the mirror before setting out for school. If a teacher finds himself generally unloved and if the forced smile hides what is watery within, he might be well advised to seek other employment. Over a period, of course, he can change. His dislike may be occasioned by his insecurity, his irritation by the mirror which the children hold up to his own faults and inadequacies, his negativism by emotional problems which he has to contend with outside school. All sorts of changes and transformations are possible over a period. But they cannot be brought about immediately by any act of will.

b *Fully developed personal relationships*   Again there is not a great deal to be said about teachers having fully developed personal relationships with their pupils. Most pupils would be too young for the degree of reciprocity which is necessary for such relationships, and to have them with every member of a class of forty would be an impossibility. Yet to confine them to a few would involve favouritism and hence unfairness. A case, however, might be made for some kind of 'positive discrimination' in this respect in the case of children who are patently deprived of such relationships because of unfortunate home circumstances. At the school level such relationships are likely to be one-sided but, nevertheless, they might be much valued by those involved in them and might be of considerable importance in the lives of particular individuals. Indeed for some pupils they might prove to be all that is remembered of school when almost all else seems to be forgotten.

It might be said that, in so far as such a relationship aids the development of a pupil, it has *ipso facto* become a role relationship. But this depends on the extent to which it is conceived of as such by the teacher. There may be a paradox here akin to the paradox of hedonism, that happiness tends to elude those who consciously pursue it. Such a relationship may in fact help the development of a pupil if the teacher does not conceive of the pupil as learning much from it. To be thought of just as an individual with a private life of one's own and not as a wayward learner might prove to be of great significance. This is the sort of relationship that a good probation officer sometimes achieves with a boy in spite of the role within which he has perforce to operate.

At boarding schools for adolescents and at universities, where some sort of tutorial system is in operation, the age of the students and the manageable numbers make such relationships much more practicable, though they are usually somewhat one-sided. They start off as embryonic personal relationships, but often develop into fully developed ones in later life. Let us, therefore, consider embryonic personal relationships.

c *Embryonic personal relationships* Our guess is that, when people talk about the importance of personal relationships in teaching, they usually have in mind the more *embryonic* type which is not at all incompatible with the teacher's role. What is advocated is that the teacher should not discharge his functions all the time in a way which is strictly dictated by his role and by general moral principles; he should, at the same time, allow glimpses of himself as a human being to slip out and be receptive to this dimension of his pupils. To use the trans-Atlantic jargon, he should 'relate' to his pupils as a human being as well as being a teacher. Our guess, also, is that this is partly what young people are demanding when they complain of the impersonality of educational institutions, and when they jib at being treated as subject-fodder or as operatives to be slotted into the occupational structure. They may, of course, be complaining of the fact that they are just being lectured at rather than being taught; that no attempt is being made to adapt what is being taught to their level of development; perhaps they may resent the fact that their teacher does not even know their names. But in so far as their complaint is about the absence of personal relationships they are not, in the main, demanding fully developed personal relationships with their teachers; they yearn for no mystic I-Thou confrontations with the professor; and, in their hearts they despise teachers who try to be with it, who copy their clothes and slang, and who have affairs with their girl friends. What they demand is that their teachers should not be so boxed up in their roles, that they should display their common humanity a bit more, and that they should evince a spontaneous interest in that of their pupils. But they also demand that they should behave with the dignity that becomes their role.

Such embryonic personal relationships can be fairly widely distributed; so there is no obvious incompatibility with the fairness that is required of a teacher. If, too, they are reasonably relaxed and spontaneous and are not too self-consciously sought, they can act as a catalyst in an educational institution. Why does this sort of thing help? Partly because it rids the atmosphere of those traces of unnecessary tension which are present when a teacher is too insecure to step out of his role and behave like a human being. (This does not mean ridding the situation of *all* tension – especially that connected with the challenge of what has to be understood or mastered.) Partly because it breaks down the barriers between teacher and taught so that the teacher is not perceived purely as a remote priest propounding somewhat esoteric doctrines. Partly because it helps to dispel the widely prevalent myth that education is something that goes on in class-rooms, laboratories, and libraries, that bears only a tenuous relationship to what goes on outside in people's private lives. Most older children carry around with them well into their teens a stereotype of a teacher as a somewhat remote figure whose main interest is not in them as people but in difficult and recondite matters, and whose main concern is to discipline them. They should not be disabused of the idea that a teacher is an authority on and devoted to initiating them into matters that may seem, prima facie, a bit beyond their ken, and that he is capable of preserving the conditions of order necessary to do this. Indeed the teacher should demonstrate this by this manifest enthusiasm and competence; but they should be disabused of the impression that he is entirely remote from them as a human being.

Embryonic personal relationships of the sort that I have been describing may do much to dispel this impression of remoteness and to convey the feeling to children that they are meeting a live human being as well as a teacher. It takes experience and judgment, however, for a teacher to behave in this way, to get the balance right between what is demanded by his role, by manners, and by morality, and what is called forth from him as a human being. It should not be thought, either, that it is *obligatory* on teachers to enter into such relationships with pupils. Many excellent teachers at the secondary or university level remain rather remote figures, showing a passion for their subject and a respect for and understanding of their pupils, but little positive interest in them as human beings. As, too, an emotional response is at the centre of such relationships, it is difficult to see how they could fall into the category of obligations. And certainly having them should never be regarded as a substitute for respecting pupils and insisting on those *impersonal* standards which are essential to the mastery of any skill or mode of experience.

It might be said, with some justice, that no teacher at the early primary stage could be successful who was so impersonal in her approach. For how could a teacher provide conditions in which very small children will learn unless she behaves towards them more like a mother towards her family than like Abelard towards the students that flocked to hear him? In this context the introduction of the image of the mother is significant; for the analysis, which we have given, has assumed that a reasonably determinate account can be given of the teacher's role in terms of treating others under the aspect of being just learners. Our analysis of 'personal relationships' has sought to distinguish them from role relationships. But the teacher's role, at the early primary stage, is much more diffuse and undifferentiated. At this level a teacher is not just treating children as learners, respecting them as individuals, treating them fairly, and so on. She is also very much concerned, as part of her role, with their welfare as individuals. She is meant to be warm and outgoing towards them, to concern herself with all their 'personal' worries and delights, to supervise their toilet, eating, and washing. She stands much more manifestly *in loco parentis* than does a teacher who is dealing with adolescents. Some kind of emotional response to them as individuals, therefore, is more or less required of her as a teacher, irrespective of whether or not it helps them to learn. Furthermore, just as the teacher's role at this level is difficult to delineate at all distinctly, so too is it impossible for the children to see her as stepping outside her role. They see her much more as a total person dealing with them, as their mother does. They do not have, at this level of their understanding of social behaviour, the concept of someone behaving towards them as an individual human being as distinct from just as a teacher. So a reciprocal response between teacher and child, under this aspect, becomes increasingly improbable as we move down towards the nursery end of the primary school.

The conclusion to be drawn from considering this end of the teaching-learning continuum is not that the analysis here given of the role of personal relationships in teaching is faulty. It is rather that it only has application to situations in which the distinctions underlying it can be made. If 'personal relationships' are defined by contrast to relationships implicit in the teacher's role the analysis will only be relevant to situations in which this kind of contrast can be made – as it manifestly can be made at the university end of the teaching-learning continuum.

4 Teaching personal relationships

So far we have been concerned with trying to get clearer about what personal relationships are and have raised questions about their compatibility with and helpfulness to teaching. But there is another obvious way of looking at them. They might be regarded not just as aids to passing on what is desirable but as things that are eminently desirable in themselves that it should be the concern of schools to pass on. Education, we have argued, is concerned with developing desirable things which involve depth and breadth of understanding. Aims of education focus attention on desirable things that ought to be developed. Hence an aim of education might be the development of personal relationships. In so far as schools are concerned with education it might well therefore be argued that they should be explicitly concerned with personal relationships as aims and not just as aids.

It would, first of all of course, have to be established that the enjoyment of personal relationships could be justified as examples of worthwhile activities. But as, in this book, we have set our face against involving ourselves with such issues of justification, we will have to assume that such a case can be made. To assume, however, that personal relationships can be regarded as valuable in themselves, is not to say anything about the extent to which the school should be concerned with them. It certainly does not require, for instance, that they should be ringed round with a halo and put on the curriculum! The point is, surely, that they arise more or less spontaneously in the context of communal activities. Teachers, by their example and by their encouragement, can do much to foster or impede them. They are surely pre-eminently the sort of things that are more effectively fostered individually by example than directly by instruction or exhortation. Like many good things in life they become spoilt if too self-consciously pursued or promoted. Teachers, too, are in a position which makes them only too vulnerable to a kind of *mauvaise foi* in this realm. They can develop one-sided personal relationships with their pupils, in which getting pupils to confide in them is a subtle way of establishing a sort of manipulatory power over them. This way of being 'child-centred' is, in our view, much more morally pernicious than the old overt authoritarianism against which the emphasis on personal relationships in teaching was, to a certain extent, a reaction.

Personal relationships, however, can manifestly be conducted at very different levels. Alf Garnett, in *Till Death Us Do Part*, inhabits a very different level of life from that of some of George Eliot's more discerning characters. The difference is largely one of depth and breadth of understanding and sensitivity, the attainment of which is characteristic of an educated person. Central to the development of this more discriminating level of personal relationships is that form of knowledge which we have previously referred to as interpersonal understanding (see Ch. 3, Sec. 2(b)). Can the school do much about developing it? Obviously something can be done in the class-room by the teaching of history, literature, and social studies with this end in view. For such enquiries directly contribute to this form of understanding. It may be aided, too, by the taking of parts in drama, and by participation in games in which the intentions and plans of others have to be divined. But probably as much is contributed indirectly by being with people whose language and whose dealings with others exemplify it.

There is, however, another crucial point about the development of this form of understanding which we can only hint at; for to discuss it adequately would require going deep into the theory of knowledge. It concerns the extent to which the development of interpersonal understanding usually proceeds *pari passu* with the forming of personal relationships. Interpersonal understanding is not a purely theoretical distanced form of knowledge. It involves imaginative reactions to what others will do, putting oneself in their shoes, seeing the world from their point of view as an arena for possible projects and predicaments. Similarly one's understanding of oneself depends in part on sensing and interpreting the reactions of others to one's own words and deeds. If people confine their dealings with others to formal and institutionalized situations they have a very limited experience on the basis of which they can interpret people's motives and innermost aspirations. A degree of emotional involvement with people of a more intimate sort is necessary before people can discover much of importance both about themselves and about others. For there is a sense in which we only know what we are when we meet others in situations which are not clearly structured in terms of the rules and roles of morality, custom, and institutional behaviour. But, of course, the quality of these non-structured reactions towards others will itself depend upon the understanding, control and sensitivity of the individuals concerned. Thus interpersonal understanding depends greatly on the data provided by concrete personal relationships, and the quality of personal relationships is enhanced by the understanding and sensitivity which individuals bring to them.

This kind of understanding and sensitivity can only come to those who have interest enough in others to enter into personal relationships with them, to really listen to what they have to say and to discern what lies behind their words, frowns, and hesitations. Too much of human intercourse lacks this stillness of mind; for most people tend to use the remarks of others only as springboards for their own self-display and self-preoccupation. But what is actually heard by those who are prepared to listen depends on the quality as well as on the quietness of their own minds. And it is education which supplies the quality.

7
Educational institutions

Introduction

The curriculum, teaching, and personal relationships are much influenced by the type of institution in which education takes place; yet nothing so far has explicitly been said about institutions, such as schools and universities, which are explicitly devoted to educational ends. This omission must be rectified; for the work of the most brilliant teacher can be nullified if the ethos of the institution in which he works is alien to all that he is trying to convey. More positively, too, we must examine what demands are to be made on institutions if they are to be concerned with education, in the specific sense which we have made explicit in this book. What type of authority structure is appropriate in them? What sort of discipline should be imposed on members? Detailed answers to such questions will depend, in part, upon considerations which are the concern of psychologists, sociologists, and practical administrators. But a philosophical exploration of the implications of a concern with *education* can do much to locate the areas in which such additional information must be sought.

I Institutions and purposes

In thinking about institutions we tend to think of some kind of building – often a forbidding one – in which a specific type of activity goes on. Asylums, schools and prisons are all institutions in this sense. A little reflection, however, should loosen the connection in our thinking between institutions and buildings. The state is an institution; yet its members are housed in every type of building. Buildings are made of materials with the imprint of mind upon them. We associate institutions with buildings because by an 'institution' we mean a body of people with a definite purpose. This often, but not always, necessitates a definite type of building to cater for it.

The purposes which are relevant to understanding institutions are not just the private, idiosyncratic purposes of its members. A man may join the police force because he wants adventure or to appear respectable; but there are many other ways in which he could satisfy these wants. In so far as he satisfies them by being a policeman, it is because he conceives of himself as a member of a group of people concerned with the maintenance of law and order. The police force, as an institution, could not be distinguished from other institutions without some reference to this dominant purpose, for the sake of furthering which men accept a body of rules and an authority structure. This welds them together into an entity which continues although the individual members change.

Institutions, for instance the state, may have more than one purpose, and, like the state, they may have come into being without anyone consciously instituting them. But these are subsidiary matters. What is central to the concept of an institution is some over-all purpose or purposes without which the behaviour of its members would be unintelligible. The purpose or purposes, which make an institution what it is, do not exist out of time and out of mind. They are generalized aims which provide a unity of purpose to an indefinite number of individuals who conceive of their actions and activities in the light of them. A policeman looks at a motorist in a different way from his fellows because he must be particularly mindful of whether or not the motorist is breaking the law. The effectiveness of an institution will depend very much on the extent to which its purpose or purposes permeate the consciousness of its members. Of course, they may be incompetent in carrying out what such purposes require. A policeman, for instance, may be unobservant or lacking in understanding of the psychology of motorists. But unless most of the members of an institution are committed to its purpose, it cannot conceivably be very effective.

Now there are factors of both an external and an internal sort that can militate against the effectiveness of an institution. These can be far more disruptive than the occasional incompetence or corruption of its members. Let us take the external factors first. Institutions have to exist in the wider context provided by the society in which they operate. It may well be that there are certain widespread valuations in a society which are so powerful that they provide motives for individual members of an institution which constantly influence and distort their behaviour as members of the institution. In a society, for instance, in which great value attaches to self-aggrandizement and individual gain, members of a religious sect may jib at things demanded of them if they involve material loss. They may shift the emphasis of their religion so that it becomes a channel through which individuals can get ahead and attain the status of the elect. Behaviour within the institution may be characterized by competitiveness and pride in position.

Internal factors can exert an equally disruptive influence. Rules may become ritualized out of all proportion to their necessity for the furthering of the purposes of the institution; an authority structure may develop a life of its own and provide power and prestige for individuals whose competence is quite unrelated to the skills necessary to administer the institution. A feeling of frustration and alienation may develop; for members may not feel that they are working together, contributing appropriately according to their ability to forward some common end.

Let us now consider the case of educational institutions bearing in mind both the importance of central purposes and the vast possibilities for disruptions and alienation deriving from external and internal sources.

2 Educational purposes and factors which militate against them

The two main institutions which are predominantly concerned with education are universities and schools. Neither of these institutions, however, are concerned exclusively with education. It might be thought, for instance, that the main concern of universities is with education. But this is an over-simple view which many university teachers would reject. They would argue that the central concern of a university is with the advancement of knowledge, whether for its own sake or to meet the needs of industry and the professions. They would extend this to include the initiation of others who can continue the advancement of knowledge. But there they would stop. They would claim that education, in so far as this involves breadth and not just depth of understanding, is the concern of schools and Liberal Arts Colleges. A lot of it, of course, will go on incidentally at universities because workers in different fields of enquiry are necessarily thrown together. So much will rub off in conversation, societies, love affairs and many other informal sorts of contact. But, it would be argued, the development of 'the whole man' is not the explicit purpose of a university.

Others, including the authors of this book, would take a more moderate position and would argue that the purpose of a university as a whole need not be equated with that of its post-graduate community. Given that students are not fully educated at school, a university must be partly concerned with developing breadth of understanding. What is distinctive, however, of a university is that this type of educational work should go on within the context of the advancement of knowledge. Those who teach undergraduates in general courses should also be doing something themselves towards advancing their own subject. This is what should be distinctive of university teaching. Schools, on the other hand, are centrally concerned with education, though they too have other concerns. At the secondary level, for instance, they are, to a certain extent, concerned with equipping people with knowledge and skills that are vocational in character. They are concerned, in other words, with training for occupations. A good school, however, will contrive such training in a way which is not inconsistent with education. This will involve the development of certain attitudes to work as well as some breadth of knowledge and understanding. Schools are also concerned with selection both for higher education and for employment. This is done partly by teachers who prepare students for examinations and write references for them, and partly by careers officers and counsellors who advise about employment and keep in touch with local firms and employment agencies. But examinations *can* also serve important educational purposes. Schools, too, are *in loco parentis* and are concerned with the health and general welfare of their pupils. At the primary level, when children can assume less responsibility for their own welfare, these concerns are more important, but they can be regarded as necessary conditions for education as well as required by a more diffuse conception of the teacher's role (see Ch. 6, Sec. 3).

Schools and universities, then, though concerned with education, are not only concerned with education. Manifestly, therefore, their concern with other purposes may militate against their effectiveness as *educational* institutions. There is also another general feature of educational institutions, especially schools, that hinders their effectiveness. Under existing conditions a large number of those who become members of them are not sympathetic to their educational purposes. 'Education', it was argued in Ch. 2, is to be understood in terms of a family of processes through which people become committed to what is valuable in a way that is illuminated by some breadth and depth of understanding. Young children not only lack knowledge and understanding; they also often lack the desire to acquire it. Perhaps all children have some innate curiosity. But, whatever the truth of this suggestion, the fact is that when they come to school, many of them seem to be without it. Maybe this is because of parental apathy towards education; maybe there is even more active discouragement at home. They are, nevertheless, compelled to attend school. So this is not an encouraging start for an institution; for its function now becomes one of converting the hostile to its purposes as well as pursuing them with the initiated. And unless it can convert a large number of the hostile it will be difficult for it to be effective as an institution. Thus, at least in the case of schools, commitment to the purposes of the institution is both an aim of the institution and a condition of its effectiveness.

This lack of fit between the purposes of educational institutions and the consciousness of many of their inmates is exacerbated by both external and internal conditions. Let us briefly sketch them in turn; for though the full description of them is properly the concern of the social scientist, they provide a necessary background for spelling out, in institutional terms, the implications of our thesis about education.

a *External* The predominant feature of Western society, to a frightening extent in North America, and to an increasing extent in Great Britain, is that it is orientated towards consumption. The all-pervading ideal is that of the possession of wealth which will open up endless opportunities for various forms of pleasure, possessions and pastimes. Jobs are seldom regarded as activities that can be pursued because of the challenge to precision and intelligence that they offer, because of their obvious contribution to the common good, because of the opportunities for fraternity and friendship that they provide. Indeed it would actually be difficult to consider a whole range of jobs in any of these lights in a modern industrial society. Rather they are looked at as necessities to be endured for the sake of the money. The ever-present question is 'Where will this get me?' – and the hazy goal in relation to which work, friendship and practical programmes are judged is that of the possibilities opened up for an increased level of consumption.

In stark contrast to this ideal of consumption stands that of an educated person who is capable of appreciating what is worthwhile in life for what there is in it as distinct from what it leads on to, who values knowledge, skill and understanding and who is capable of seeing a car not just as a convenience to aid his consumption or as a status symbol, but as a product of skill and ingenuity, with some aesthetic grace, as an object with a history and with potentialities for human good and ill. He is a person who can delight in a job well done because of the opportunities for skill, creation and precision that it offers, who can enjoy people because there is nothing more interesting to man than man, and who can pursue knowledge for its own sake, or create things because of his desire to objectify feelings that he cannot put into words, without nagging thoughts about where such activities are going to get him. For, after all, where ultimately is there to get?

An institution, however, that is ostensibly dedicated to education has an uphill task in such a society; for both teachers and students alike are bound to be affected by the motivations of the wider society. Teachers may tend to take a purely instrumental view of their job and to be more concerned with their own advancement than with education; for they may be preoccupied with increasing their status and level of consumption by judicious moves and bargaining. Loyalty to their institution is of minor importance when compared with concern for their own careers. They will also tend to employ incentives to get students to work that are manifestly related to the level of consumption, namely success in examinations. And the students themselves will tend to view their 'education' in the same light, as a series of hurdles that have to be surmounted if a well-paid job is to be obtained. Such instrumental considerations are not, of course, entirely inappropriate for either teachers or students. The question is how much emphasis is given to them and how much they dominate the life of an educational institution.

The content of the curriculum may become, in a similar way, very closely related to the instrumental order. For instance business men or governments may provide finance for programmes designed explicitly for types of employment, and because one of the obvious subsidiary purposes of schools and universities is to prepare people for work, the institutions may welcome such finance. And there is nothing inappropriate, of course, in centring learning on practical tasks. The crucial question, however, is whether such programmes are narrowly conceived exercises in training or whether they are also vehicles for education. There is also the question of whether they are taught in such a way that they encourage a purely instrumental attitude towards learning.

b *Internal* The pressures from the outside which make identification with the purposes of an educational institution difficult may be reinforced by the institution's own authority structure. Suppose, for instance, that a university is organized by a predominantly non-academic administration who run it rather like a business and influence unduly academic appointments and salary differentials on academically irrelevant grounds. Suppose that a professor runs his department in an authoritarian way and does not involve his staff in decisions about matters that vitally concern it. Or suppose that a headmaster of a school rules it autocratically, playing one member of staff off against another, and allowing no scope for genuine democratic discussion. Suppose that decisions in institutions are taken secretly and announced without opportunities for criticisms and objections. In institutions of this sort it is most unlikely that there will be much involvement in the purposes of the institution. Yet without such involvement it is equally unlikely that most of its members will be able to put up much resistance to the motivations from outside, which will make them cynical, and self-seeking.

Students in such institutions may indeed come to feel alienated from its avowed purposes. They are there ostensibly to be educated but, in fact, they may think they are only there to get their foot firmly on the ladder of the occupational structure. The institution is meant, in part at any rate, to be run for their benefit as well as for that of society generally; perhaps some kindly counsellor or careers master advises them and tries to help them get on the right track. But it is all very paternalistic. They do not feel that it is their institution. At least Thomas Arnold, who so influenced the much maligned English Public Schools tradition, grasped the point that if the boys themselves could be made largely responsible for the disciplinary and recreational side of their life, they would feel some involvement in the institution, even if the authority system, which the boys themselves administered, was autocratic in structure.

Of course increased participation in the running of an educational institution is not the only way of encouraging commitment to its purposes on the part of those who are initially hostile or indifferent to them. Institutions that are paternalistically organized sometimes manage this through a process of identification with some of their authority figures. The admiration felt for the skilled and the experienced can be channelled into enthusiasm for the ideals and pursuits which they are trying to pass on. This process of transmission, however, operates much more powerfully at the lower than it does at the upper end of the age range. At the upper end, in higher education and in the latter stages of secondary education, it is less powerful than it used to be because of the increased hostility of young people towards any form of paternalism. Indeed a serious problem of modern industrialized societies is this gap between the generations which militates generally against learning from the experienced.

What, then, is an appropriate authority structure for educational institutions? For there is a danger that authority in general will be confused with authoritarianism and that people will be persuaded that the only alternative to paternalism is a plebiscite of the pupils. Our argument will be that neither of these extremes is rationally defensible as providing an appropriate system of administration for academic institutions. Genuine participation must be achieved in a way which is appropriate to the peculiar purposes of schools and universities. Again we claim that philosophical analysis can disclose a middle way between traditional paternalism and the progressive reaction against it.

This middle way, we argue, can be set out by exploring what is demanded of schools and universities *in so far as their purposes are educational*. We have admitted the existence of other purposes for both types of institutions but we will ignore the implications introduced by them. In particular we will ignore the difference at the university level between the advancement of knowledge and the transmission of knowledge. We shall argue that, in so far as universities and schools are concerned with the advancement and transmission of public forms of knowledge, this has certain implications for their authority structure, for the role of the teacher, and for the type of discipline which is desirable. Looking at these institutions from the perspective provided by their concern with education will provide us with a rational approach to the problems of authority. If authority is approached in this way there is hope that universities and schools will become more effective as educational institutions.

3 Authority and educational institutions

Institutions, it has been argued, involve distinct purposes. They also involve rules which members have to accept in order to pursue such purposes effectively. Ideally all such rules should be closely related to its purposes or should be part of the more general moral and legal code of the community. But, in practice, arbitrary arrangements grow up, especially under a paternalistic system, which assume an importance out of all proportion to their rational justification. It may well be, therefore, that when progressives attack authority in educational institutions, they are confusing such needless excesses of authority with authority itself. But what is authority? Let us briefly consider its nature and then relate this analysis to the special position of educational institutions.

a *The nature of authority* Institutions, it has been said, involve rules as well as purposes; but behind the idea of a rule stands the idea of there being a right and a wrong way of doing things, and there can always be a question about what is the right way. In the case of what we call moral rules the right way of doing things depends upon the reasons that can be produced for it; and it is assumed that any reasonable person would be able to concur with such relevant considerations. But there are spheres of human life in which another type of procedure is necessary – that of an appeal to authority. In disputes about the rules of golf, for instance, the matter is referred to the ultimate authority, the Royal and Ancient. Similarly in the community generally a legal system has developed, whose function it is to determine what rules are ultimately to be binding and enforced in the area over which it extends. This is a system for determining what the rules are to be, and for interpreting them in particular cases; there is also the necessity for enforcing rules, which is another function of authority. Whenever there is a second-order structure for determining in general what is correct or incorrect, for interpreting this in particular cases, and for enforcing it we are in the realm of authority.

Authority, too, manifests itself in the sphere of assertions as well as in the sphere of rules. We talk of someone as being *an* authority on the Aztecs; oracles are consulted; experts give authoritative opinions; and popes makes pronouncements on matters of doctrine. Typical figures of authority are judges, umpires, policemen, professors and priests. Such people are accorded a right to decide, command, enforce or pronounce. In brief, authority is present when something is correct or to be done because an individual, or body of men, who has been given the right, says so.

b   *The rationalization of authority*   Historically speaking authority systems have been regarded very much as part of the order of things. People were accorded a right to command because they were born into certain families and traditions bestowed upon them this right. Gradually, however, with the development of reason and individualism, it came to be realized that authority systems are alterable and not part of the order of things like the seasons and the movement of the planets. Not only was the right of certain families challenged; fundamental questions were also asked about the institution of authority itself. For *prima facie* it seemed an affront to the freedom and dignity of a rational man that he should have to obey orders given by another man and submit to a system in which what was correct and true was settled by appeal to another man or body of men. These questionings made way for modern theories of democracy and a more rational approach to the problem of authority. As a result, in the sphere of social control, where people were regarded as being *in* authority, paternalism gradually passed away in this country. But it was not replaced by anarchy. Rather authority became rationalized. The form of authority became more closely related to the reasons for having it, such as security or the protection of individual rights, and people were increasingly appointed to offices on relevant grounds, such as their ability to perform the tasks in question rather than on irrelevant grounds such as birth and family connections. This took time. It was not until Gladstone's time, for instance, that competitive examinations for the Civil Service were introduced.

This transition to a more rational acceptance of authority took place, in part, because even to those who believe fervently in freedom, the case for having some form of authority in the sphere of social control is overwhelmingly strong. The case depends upon a combination of certain empirical facts about men and the general desirability of the continuance of a form of society in which free-dom, fairness and the consideration of people's interests are accepted as desirable conditions of social life. It is a general empirical fact that men are born with unequal endowment. It also seems to be generally the case that those who are stronger and cleverer tend to dominate those who are not so endowed. If, therefore, men were permitted unlimited freedom to do what they liked, it would not be the case that all would in fact be free or able to do it. Rather the strong would constrain the weak. Con-straints of an impersonal sort are therefore necessary to get rid of these more personalized forms of constraint, and to guarantee conditions of security. An authority system, which formulates, applies, and enforces the rule of law, is necessary to protect the weak from the arbitrary exercise of power. Its justification is in terms of freedom as well as in terms of the interest of all; for without such protection only the strong would in fact be free and able to do what they wanted – largely at the expense of others. And they will not remain in this favoured position for ever. So all must accept the levelling constraint of law in order to be rid of more arbitrary constraints. Authority is therefore necessary in order that freedom shall be a reality, as well as that people's basic interests shall be safeguarded.

In the sphere of knowledge, however, where we talk of a person being *an* authority, the rational case for authority might not seem to be so strong. If, therefore, institutions, such as schools and universities, which are concerned with the transmission of know-ledge, seem paternalistic to their members, it might be tempting to conclude that there is no case for anyone being an authority. After all, it might be argued, what is true or false does not depend, in the end, on the word of any man. It depends on reasons which any rational man can grasp. Why, therefore, should we attempt even to rationalize authority in this sphere? Maybe there is a case for having people *in* authority in such institutions in order to per-mit them to function peacefully. But why have authorities concerned with the transmission of knowledge as well? And why put them in authority rather than administrators whose concern should be only the rule of law and the day to day running of such institutions?

The case for institutionalizing authorities in the sphere of know-ledge depends upon the empirical fact that men take a very long time to develop all their faculties and that their survival depends largely on their ability to master a vast heritage of knowledge and skill which is necessary to maintain a complex society. Civilized men do not grow up overnight like mushrooms; they become civilized by being brought up by others who are civilized. And this means an important role for the experienced. Whether they like it or not the experienced must function for a time as authorities and this type of authority must be institutionalized if it is to be effective. This means families and, usually, educational institutions.

The need for special educational institutions has become imperative because human knowledge has now become so complex and specialized that no man can possibly know all that needs to be known for a modern industrialized society to be perpetuated. The family can no longer fulfil this educational role; for authorities or experts in the various branches of knowledge, e.g. medicine, engineering, statistics, must be trained. Of course such authorities are often mistaken; so their pronouncements must be treated with a tinge of scepticism and caution. They are only *provisional* authorities, not ultimate authorities; for there are no such final arbiters in the sphere of knowledge. The crucial point about them is that their authority derives from their special training and mastery of the relevant sphere of knowledge, on their success in getting things right in a sphere where what is right or true does not depend on the pronouncements of any individual, but on reasons and evidence that any one can, in principle, grasp. The advancement and transmission of such specialized knowledge and skill is largely the concern of schools and universities. For teachers are put in authority in such institutions because they are assumed to be authorities on those bodies of knowledge and skill which are essential to the form of life of a community. Let us, therefore, consider in more detail what a rational structure of authority would be in such institutions.

c *The rationalization of authority in educational institutions* It has been argued that, although there is a prima facie antagonism between authority and the use of reason, a rational case can be made for authority in institutions if its exercise is clearly related to the purposes of the institution and if staff are appointed on relevant grounds to discharge various responsibilities on the community's behalf. Universities and schools are centrally concerned with the advancement and transmission of various forms of skill and knowledge; so it follows that these overriding purposes should determine the structure of authority within such institutions. What would be the implications of trying to relate the authority-structure to these purposes?

The first implication of this overriding purpose is in what might be termed the principle of academic autonomy. This principle maintains that, whether institutions are financed by the state or by private individuals, those who are responsible for the development and transmission of knowledge must have freedom to do this; for, as was argued by J. S. Mill in his essay *On Liberty*, the pursuit of truth would be impossible without insistence on the principle of freedom. Once academics give up their right to determine their own lines of research and teaching, once heterodox opinions are stifled, once research or teaching which are politically inconvenient or embarrassing to businessmen are suppressed, the advancement of knowledge will suffer. Any institution, therefore, which is centrally concerned with the advancement or transmission of knowledge must insist on such freedom.

The second implication is that of the provisional authority of academics. It was argued in Ch. 4 that the differentiation of knowledge into distinct forms is not an arbitrary matter. There are distinctive concepts, truth-criteria and methodologies which anyone must master who is to have an opinion which is to be reckoned with. There is also a body of knowledge, which has to be mastered, which has been built up by and can be criticized by people who have been trained to work in this form of knowledge. It takes time and considerable experience to master these forms of knowledge, so that a person is in a position to judge and criticize in an informed way. This means that there must be provisional authorities in the different forms and fields of knowledge with which universities and schools are concerned. Their job is to hand on an inheritance in such a way that others can come to criticize it and eventually dispense with their teachers. They must exercise their authority in such a way that another generation can learn to live without them. In order to get on the inside of a form of knowledge a certain course of study is required. On the content of this course, the opinion of the academics is the most relevant one. At a later stage, of course, when students have attained some competence, there should be plenty of room for options, for discussion about priorities, and for exploring new fields. But this presupposes that students already have the basic equipment to make informed choices.

What are the more concrete implications of these abstract principles for universities and schools? Obviously, first of all that academics should decide on lines of research and on syllabuses. Secondly that they shall have the main responsibility for appointing their colleagues. And thirdly that they shall have the responsibility for selecting and examining students. For they alone possess the specialized knowledge necessary for deciding issues of this sort. The details of how these implications are worked out will depend, to a certain extent, on local conditions and on whether the institution is a school or a university. Syllabuses of schools, and examinations, for instance, may be the joint responsibility of academics from universities and schools. Administrators and representatives of the local community may sit on appointment committees. There may be student representation on academic boards. And so on. All this is reasonable enough provided that the academics have the major say about what is to be taught and who is to teach.

Students at university level often argue that they are the consumers and that they should therefore have the major say in academic decisions. It is unfortunate that they should be so corrupted by the consumer-network that they should press their claims by means of this grossly inappropriate model. They fail to appreciate, too, that, if this model is pressed home, it can be argued even more cogently that the general public and beneficient business men are the real consumers; for they put up most of the money and have a right to expect a neatly packaged product at the end of the 'educational process'.

Another argument that students sometimes put forward for the 'democratization' of educational institutions is that this is the only form of government that is appropriate in a democratic society. Schools and universities should not be governed only by the wise, like Plato's ideal state. There are, however, two flaws in this argument which can be exposed without exploring all the ambiguities in the concept of 'democracy'. There is, firstly, the obvious point that many of the inmates of educational institutions are of too immature years to qualify as full citizens. Secondly, the state is not an institution which has a dominant purpose connected with specialized matters on which there are manifest authorities. The state is an institution with many purposes – the provision of security, the protection of rights, arbitration between conflicting interests, and the maintenance of minimum standards of welfare, to mention only a few. The implementation of such purposes depends as much on moral decision as it does on technical knowledge. And on moral matters there are no manifest authorities. Plato thought that only the philosopher kings properly understand moral matters. If he had been right about the status of moral knowledge the case for his aristocracy of the wise would be very difficult to answer. But schools and universities *do* have much more specific purposes connected with the advancement and transmission of specialized forms of knowledge on which there *are* authorities. The ordinary man's opinions about physics, engineering, botany, sociology, etc., are of little more significance than those of the student just embarking on such studies, or of the patient going to a doctor for a cure. It is interesting, in this context, to recall that Plato regarded the state, to a large extent, as an educational institution.

There is, however, an important distinction to be made which is suggested by this argument from democratic practices. It concerns the different types of decisions that have to be taken on educational matters. It has been argued in Ch. 2 that many different aims are possible in education which are compatible with the general aim of the development of knowledge and understanding. On matters of priority between possible aims, or between competing forms of development, the view of the academic is not necessarily much more discerning than that of the ordinary enlightened citizen or of the sensible student. For moral and political judgments play a crucial role in these sorts of decisions and, as has already been argued, the case for authorities on moral matters is not a strong one. In this respect moral knowledge is very unlike science, history, and mathematics. Such types of decision, also, are very often linked with wider social and economic issues. There will therefore be many types of decision, such as are taken by governing bodies, as distinct from those of academic boards, on which the view of academics is only one view that must be heard along with that of other interested parties such as students and representatives of the general public. Obviously, too, on matters such as finance, buildings, and links between educational institutions and the wider community, academics have no special expertise. So these too are spheres for joint decision-making between academics, students, and representatives of the general public.

It is impossible to be much more specific about who should decide what in educational institutions; for there are so many variations in the ways in which such institutions are organized. All we are suggesting is a rationale underlying decision-making derivative from the central purposes of educational institutions. We have argued that academics should have the major say on matters intimately concerned with the advancement and transmission of specialized knowledge. This, however, is not to suggest that on these matters they should be immune from criticism from others or that they should not consult with students. On the broad lines of syllabuses, for instance, and on methods of examining there is no earthly reason why they should not consult with the students, whom they actually teach, in order to arrive at more sensible decisions. Academics too often go on hunches about what students think without taking the trouble to find out. A particular case in point is teaching methods, and the organization of courses. Academics should be able to call on an established body of specialized knowledge which would enable them to predict the probable outcomes of adopting lecturing, seminars, or individual tutorial techniques. They should know the strength and weakness of various technical aids. And so on. In fact there is, at the moment, no such body of specialized knowledge. It would, therefore, seem obvious sense to involve students in discussions about alternative ways of teaching and learning. For, apart from the fact that much can be learnt from such discussions, if learners as well as teachers come to regard learning as a joint enterprise, the amount of learning will probably increase, as well as commitment to the purposes of the institution. This applies at the school as well as at the university level.

Criticism and consultation, however, are one thing; ultimate responsibility for decisions is quite another. Once academics give up their ultimate right to determine the content of what is to be taught, and the ways in which they are going to teach it, they will in time become the hired lackeys of the community, not authorities on its stock of knowledge. Their own freedom and thoroughness in the transmission of knowledge will be in jeopardy. They may find that they are forbidden to teach the economic interpretation of history or to dwell on facts about a nation's past that are not too palatable to the public; or they may find that they are banned from teaching the theories of a bourgeois individualist thinker such as Freud. For the public, politicians and university administrators could equally well claim that they should determine what is taught as well as the students who are subsidized by the public.

On all sorts of other matters, however, which are not intimately connected with the advancement and transmission of specialized knowledge, there is every reason why there should be joint decision-making rather than consultation. Obvious examples would be matters to do with discipline, residential arrangements, common room and refectory facilities, and so on. There are other spheres, too, for instance recreational activities, clubs, and societies where students have for a long time managed their affairs and consulted members of staff as they think fit.

Ideally, at the level of higher education, there should be a commitment on the part of all, students and staff alike, to the purposes for which an academic community exists – the development of knowledge, whether theoretical or practical, the enlargement of the understanding, and the enhancement of sympathy and sensitivity. This is made difficult at the moment by the paternalistic attitude of many of the staff, the secrecy with which their decisions are shrouded, and their combination of defensiveness and authoritarianism towards the students. It is made difficult by the predominantly instrumental attitude of many students towards learning, which they pick up at school and in society at large, and which is enhanced by too much grading. But an equally important factor in this lack of involvement in the purposes of the community is the absence of any rational policy about consultation, criticism, and decision-making. It is no good expecting people to feel committed to the purposes of an institution if con-crete provision is lacking which permits appropriate participation and undistorted communication. Each institution has to work out its own arrangements in the light of its own idiosyncracies in a way which grants students more rights to representation without either threatening the academic freedom of the teacher or denying the different status of staff and students in relation to the advance-ment and transmission of knowledge. In brief the authority struc-ture of educational institutions must be rationalized by adjusting it more sensibly to their purposes. Academic paternalism is as inappropriate as the proffered alternative of student power; for neither spring from any thought-out attempt to devise an authority structure appropriate to the specific purposes of educational institu-tions.

At the school level this difference in status between staff and students is obviously more marked than at university level. But the difference is only one of degree depending on the age of the pupils and the types of responsibility that they are competent to carry. In English schools the headmaster has an astonishing degree of autonomy; so it is more or less up to him what he does about involving staff and pupils in decision-making. Hence the scandalous state of affairs which still exists in many English schools in which the headmaster does not even involve the staff in decision-making, let alone the pupils. It is almost worse if lip-service is paid to democratic procedures by calling meetings and ostensibly consult-ing other members of staff while in fact the head is making all the decisions. It is of cardinal importance in democratic procedure that people should know whether they have been summoned like retainers for 'advice and consent' or whether they are members of a meeting which has real competence to make decisions. A great deal of cynicism and apathy is bred if some formal façade of democracy is preserved whilst all the important decisions are taken elsewhere. This is as likely to produce alienation from an institution as more straightforward and less manipulatory types of pater-nalism. For the case for participation in the running of an institu-tion by those who do most of the work is not merely one of right; it is also one of public interest. An institution will surely be much more effective in carrying out its purposes if there is communica-tion between its staff and a sense of shared responsibility for its destiny.

The types of argument so far used in discussing the place of student participation in educational institutions might equally well have been used if we had been considering the case for worker par-ticipation in the running of a factory. A dimension of argument has been overlooked which is peculiarly appropriate to educational as distinct from other sorts of institutions. This is a consideration of what a form of organization contributes to the education of its members. In other words, in a school we must not only ask to what extent its organization should be democratic; we must also ask what contribution it makes to education for democracy. Now a great part of such education surely takes place on an apprenticeship basis. Good chairmen and secretaries of committees are not born; they become so by a combination of practice and learning from the experienced. Similarly taking part sensibly in a democratic debate requires more than general knowledge and an ability to criticize arguments which can be learnt from books; neither is it a skill that flowers miraculously when children grow up. It is the product of training and practice. How can young people be expected to acquire such skills if they are given no opportunities to practise them? Teachers and youth-leaders who have tried committees and parliaments often complain that the same sorts of points keep on coming up with each new batch of members; the same explanations and justifications have to be put forward; often the same sorts of mistakes are made. But what else is to be expected? And could not the same sort of point be made about classroom lessons? In matters which are not of central concern to the development of an educational institution efficiency may have, at times, to be sacrificed slightly in the cause of education.

Pupil participation in running a school will depend on so many variables that it is impossible to do much more than sketch general guide-lines derivative from the purpose of the institution. It will depend on whether it is a day-school or a boarding-school, whether or not it has an effective house-system, the age of the pupils, the size of the school and so on. Participation of pupils in decision-making about academic matters such as types of courses and teaching methods is likely to be much more limited than at the university level; but there is a great deal of scope for joint decision-making as well as for consultation about school rules and discipline, out-of-school activities, and countless other matters. In too many schools an atmosphere is generated that makes the school seem like a shop or a dispensary where the staff lay on what they think is good for the customers in a way which will appeal to them. The pupils do not feel that they are involved in a joint enterprise. Any institutional arrangements which can help to generate this feeling of involvement, which are consistent with the academic autonomy and provisional authority of teachers, are surely to be welcomed.

d *The rationalization of the authority of the school-teacher* At the school level the rationalization of authority is of particular relevance to the position of the teacher in relation to his pupils.

For the traditional conception of the teacher as a benevolent despot is no more appropriate than the progressive conception of the teacher as a child-grower. In so far as the teacher is put in authority by the community he has to administer and enforce rules; but such rules, apart from general moral rules and the legal rules of the community, should be justifiable by reference either to particular educational purposes in the class-room or to the effective administration of the institution as a whole. To delight in giving orders and in making rules for their own sake, or to provide backing for rules by appealing only to status, is to be authoritarian; this is only one way of exercising authority and not a way which is rationally defensible. On the other hand to refuse to enforce rules or to maintain conditions of order necessary for education to proceed is to be irrational in another way; for it is to refuse to take the means necessary to a desired end. Some progressives, who shrink from the use of authority, because they confuse it with being authoritarian, in fact exert control by more subtle psychological techniques. They say things like 'Now children, we would like to see the room tidy before we go home, wouldn't we?' or they use their own personal magnetism to charm children into compliance with their wishes. It is questionable whether such techniques are rationally any more defensible than the overt authoritarianism of the traditional teacher.

In order to keep the enterprise of education going, especially in its early stages, certain minimal conditions of order have to be maintained. Decisions have to be made about how an institution is to function; order has to be preserved, and in doing this certain devices connected with authority, such as issuing commands and requests, are in place, as well as more rational methods of persuasion. But if commands are employed they too can be rationalized, or related strictly to the task in hand, and not delighted in purely as an expression of status or because of a liking to bend others to one's will. The teacher, therefore, who is determined to use his reason, has to learn to be in authority without being authoritarian.

Whether or not a teacher behaves in an authoritarian way it is very probable that some children will revere and admire him as an authority figure and identify with him. Any teacher with an elementary knowledge of psychology will expect this and will be foolish to ignore or deplore a fact of life that may be both a boon and a bane to him. It will be a boon if he uses this a-rational bond to bring about a transfer of children's interest in him to an interest in those worthwhile things that he is trying to transmit. It will be a bane if he enjoys the feeling of power over others so much that he prolongs the period of dependence which provides him with such splendid opportunities to pontificate.

The distinction, which we have made in Ch. 2, between a public mode of experience and a particular content built up and criticized by means of it does much to provide not only a way out of this situation of dependence on an authority, but also a rationale for the position of the teacher as *an* authority. The traditional teacher was thought to be an authority on content – on capes and bays and the dates of the Kings of England. The progressive teacher, on the other hand, was thought of as being more of an authority on the development of children. In our account of 'development' in Ch. 3, in terms of the differentiation of distinct modes of experience, we attempted a synthesis between the subject-centred and the child-centred approaches. Such an emphasis on development of modes of experience as aims of education does much to provide a more rational account of the teacher's position as an authority. For on this view he is a person who has achieved some kind of mastery of a public mode of experience that anyone else can in principle master; his task is to stimulate these forms of development so that his pupils will eventually have the conceptual equipment to manage on their own.

Teachers are, therefore, what we have called provisional authorities; for their job is not just to hand on a body of knowledge, but also to initiate another generation into those public modes of experience by means of which it has been developed and by means of which it can be criticized and revised. In the later stages of education, therefore, teachers should regard themselves as teaching badly if they do not find that some students begin to challenge them and pick holes in what they say. They must teach in such a way that their students regard them very much as only provisional authorities who can be dispensed with as they grow older. The good teacher is therefore a person who is always working himself out of a job.

4 Discipline and punishment

In the popular mind the necessity of maintaining necessary conditions of order in a school is connected with discipline and punishment. In the context of the general thesis of this chapter it is necessary to deal briefly and selectively with these highly controversial topics; for in schools one of the most potent sources of a feeling of alienation from the purposes of the institution is the punishment system. For this often corroborates the conviction of the pupils that education is something which is imposed on them from outside by the custodians of a coercive corporation. It is therefore important to spell out the kind of discipline that is appropriate for an institution concerned with *education*. It is important, however, to distinguish 'punishment' from 'discipline' punishment being just one method of preserving discipline.

a *Discipline* 'Discipline', etymologically speaking, is derived from the Latin word 'disco' which means 'I learn'. The root idea is that of submission to rules that structure what has to be learnt – e.g. the rules to be observed in swinging a golf-club, in speaking grammatically, or in controlling one's impulses. They may be rules which are immanent in a *way of thinking*, e.g. those of scientific, mathematical or historical thinking. They may be rules which are *necessary* for learning something, such as rules about practice, revision, trying out different examples. And so on. Education necessarily involves learning, and all learning involves discipline in one or more of the above senses. So education necessarily involves discipline.

It is usual to distinguish self-imposed discipline from discipline that it is imposed by others. This distinction, too, is important in the context of the thesis of this book. For self-imposed discipline was the type which was set up as an ideal by the progressives in contrast to that which was imposed by the authoritarian disciplinarian of the traditional school. Obviously our sympathy is very much with the progressives in this; for the notion of self-discipline is very closely connected with the ideal of autonomy which was implicit in their approach. And in Ch. 3 autonomy was cited as an example of a human excellence that could function as an end-point of human development. It is worthwhile, therefore, to attempt to get a bit clearer about what is involved in self-discipline; for it is not an entirely perspicuous notion.

Discipline is usually thought to be self-imposed if conforming to rules or standards is accepted by the individual as either constitutive of or a means to doing something that he wants to do or thinks desirable. Examples of the constitutive type of discipline would be cases where children are delighted by the sound of music and set about learning to play themselves, when they are intrigued by a town or building and set about finding out more about it, or when they become fascinated by the habits of animals or the workings of a machine and set to work to understand why and how. Examples of the self-imposed means-end type of discipline would be when an individual decides to submit to a diet and to regular exercise in order to keep healthy or when he learns French in order to enjoy himself abroad.

These cases of self-discipline are thought to be educationally desirable because the submission to rules springs from the individual's own decisions in which some kind of autonomy is displayed. They are contrasted with cases when the acceptance of rules springs from other people's desires – those of teachers, parents and the peer-group. This is somewhat of an over-simplification though; for the child's desires and decisions are involved in these cases too. He wants to avoid the disapproval of parents and teachers and the censure of the peer-group. It would be inadequate also to characterize these cases as those where the desire is always to avoid something unpleasant; for surely bribing children to learn things by offering them prizes is an externally imposed form of discipline just as much as coercing them by threats of punishment. Perhaps what is central to the 'externality' is the suggestion that the child is being made to do what *others* want by manipulating him and playing on his desires and fears. His options are so closed up that he is confronted with a kind of Hobson's choice.

But what of cases where a child models himself on a teacher in some respect that the teacher is not particularly concerned to make a feature of his teaching – his use of very neat, small writing, for instance? Is this a case of externally imposed discipline? For the hypothesis is that the child does not discipline himself to write neatly because he wants to please the teacher but because he admires the teacher and models himself on him. This is a very important process of transmission.

This intermediary type of case suggests another feature of the type of discipline that is of most educational value – that of the absence of an *artificial* connection between what is wanted and the submission to rules. In the obvious cases of imposed discipline the connection between what is wanted by the child and what the teacher wants him to learn is artificially created. Prizes and the pain involved in censure and punishment present very general objects of desire or aversion that are tacked on in an artificial way to what has to be learnt. So in learning what has to be learnt the child is learning an irrelevant connection as well as developing an instrumental attitude. In the cases of self-imposed discipline, on the other hand, the connection between the submission to rules and what is wanted is not so artificial. The child is not therefore picking up a lot of irrelevant associations while he is subjecting himself to rules. Rules of diet and taking exercise are means to health because of facts about the body; learning some biological or mechanical theory is intrinsically connected with the particular sort of curiosity which is aroused in the child who is fascinated by animals or machines. The case of copying the handwriting of an admired person is an intermediary case because the connection between the handwriting and the object of admiration is very close. We do not admire people in the abstract, but for certain of their qualities. Admiration for a person is intrinsically connected with *some* of his qualities, which perhaps extends to his handwriting. Indeed a child might be drawn to a teacher *because* of his handwriting amongst other qualities. But even if a teacher is admired for other qualities and the child's emulation extends to qualities distinct from those which originally form the basis of his admiration, the connection is not nearly so artificial as in the other obvious cases of externally imposed discipline.

It should not be thought, however, that self-discipline is only valuable as a means which is intrinsically related to what is thought desirable. As has already been pointed out it has a close connection with autonomy, which has been suggested as a human excellence, and hence as an educational end. There are other excellences, too, such as integrity and courage, which manifestly involve self-discipline; for they are virtues which have to be exercised in the face of counter-inclinations. Self-discipline enters into such excellences as a constituent in them, not as a means to them.

There is also the point that what we have called public modes of experience, such as science, mathematics, and philosophy, which, we argued in Ch. 3, are preconditions of excellences such as autonomy, are themselves often called 'disciplines'. Presumably they are so-called because the learner submits himself to the rules which are implicit in them. His consciousness becomes gradually structured by their procedures. He thus adopts an increasingly disciplined approach. But this is part of the characterization of an educated man. Such discipline is constitutive of what is to be aimed at in education. It is not just to be regarded as a means to it. Indeed a closer examination of the importance of 'discipline' in education would be one way of revealing the limitations of the concept of 'means-to-an-end' in describing the processes of education.

So far 'discipline' has been considered as intimately connected with specific things that have to be learnt. More usually, perhaps, in a school context it is used to refer to the maintenance of general conditions of order without which nothing can be effectively learnt. It is connected with children being brought, by various forms of persuasion and coercion, to accept rules forbidding them to make too much noise, to fight in class, to be rude to the teacher, and so on. Without such general conditions of order teaching cannot go on, though the type of order required should be related rationally to what is being learnt, the number and age of the children, the amount of space in the class-room and other such variables.

Discipline, then, of one form or another is either conceptually or empirically necessary to education. It is conceptually necessary to it in that some forms of discipline are part of our understanding of 'education' because of the connections between 'education' and 'learning' and 'learning' and 'discipline'. It is empirically necessary for the enterprise of education to proceed. But what about punishment? Is that necessary to education in either of these senses?

b *Punishment* Punishment is often confused with discipline because it is a device to which teachers and parents often resort in order to maintain discipline. It is therefore a frequent empirical condition of discipline. It is, however, conceptually distinct from discipline. 'Punishment', in its central cases, has at least three logically necessary conditions. (For distinction between logically and empirically necessary conditions see back to pp. 4-5.)

i It must involve the intentional infliction of pain or of some kind of unpleasantness.

ii This must be inflicted on an offender as a consequence of a breach of rules.

iii It must be inflicted by someone in authority.

Discipline, on the other hand, is not necessarily painful, neither does it necessarily emanate from someone in authority. Regular physical exercise is an example of discipline, but need satisfy neither of these conditions. Discipline is conceptually related to the second condition; for a breach of rules *is* a breach of discipline. It is this overlap which leads to the confusion between the two concepts.

There is another type of confusion in relation to this condition which is also worth mentioning. Psychologists often speak about the use of 'punishment' in the context of learning rules, skills, and so on. This is appropriately so called if pain is inflicted in order to bring a back-slider back to the mark, if he breaks a rule, but it is not really appropriately called 'punishment' if it is inflicted to teach a child a rule with which he is not yet familiar. If, for instance, rules of arithmetic are taught by a process of negative reinforcement this is not, strictly speaking, punishment. It is using pain as an extrinsic aid to learning. Punishment proper, however, *may* function as a device that aids moral learning. By experiencing a sharp shock for a breach of a rule, a boy may be brought to his senses. He may grasp vividly the importance which the community attaches to the rule. Punishment here is a dramatic way of underlining a rule, of marking it out as important.

This introduces the question of the justification of punishment; for it is often assumed in an educational context that the reform of the individual offender is the only good reason for punishment in the case of breaches of social rules. As there is little evidence that punishment has such beneficial results it is often concluded that it should be dispensed with in schools. This is a gross over-simplification; for, leaving aside its underlining function, the basic case for punishment both in schools, and in the community generally, is not as a reformative but as a deterrent measure. Penalties are attached to the breach of rules in order to uphold the rule of law, to deter possible offenders as well as to deal with actual ones. The utilitarian case is that less harm is done if small doses of pain are inflicted on offenders than would be done if the rule of law was not enforced. A punishment system is working best, therefore, when it rarely has to be used, when the *threat* of penalties is sufficient to deter possible offenders. As on the utilitarian view pain is the most palpable evil, it is always regrettable when penalties have actually to be imposed. Punishment is therefore a necessary mischief, the lesser of two evils.

The relevance of this to the school situation is obvious enough. Discipline, in the sense of general conditions of order, has to be maintained if teaching is to proceed. Ideally this can be maintained by the enthusiasm and efficiency of the teacher and the general commitment to learning on the part of the pupils. Unfortunately, however, such conditions do not always obtain. The teacher may not be very inspiring; there may be a group of pupils who are determined to disrupt proceedings; or they may be so used to this way of enforcing discipline that they do not take anyone seriously who refuses to employ it. The teacher then has to have recourse to punishment. If he does so he will have to employ forms of punishment that are both *unpleasant* and *predictable*; for, if he does not, punishment will fail to function as a deterrent – which is the only good reason for employing it. It would be nice if forms of punishment could be devised which had both these qualities and also had a reformative effect on children. As, however, it has yet to be shown that many types of punishment actually do children any good, at least the teacher must devise deterrents that do not do them any obvious harm.

The unfortunate result, however, of punishment on the individual is that, although it may not do him any harm, it is very likely to alienate him further from the purposes of the school. It reinforces his view of the school as a corporation whose main concern is to coerce him into doing things which he does not want to do. The teacher, therefore, must pursue a two-dimensional policy. On the one hand he must be just and maintain the rule of law impartially; on the other hand he must not only respect the individual offender but also convey to him the sense that he is not unsympathetic to him as a human being, that he understands his point of view and his personal problems. He has to act, in other words, both as a person in authority and as a human being. The extent to which he can effectively do this will depend on the sort of personal relationships he has with his pupils, in the senses which were distinguished in the last chapter.

5 Conclusion

Much ground has been rather cursorily covered in this chapter in order to outline a predicament, which is that of the alienation from the purposes of educational institutions of so many who are members of them, who are in them but not of them. Emphasis has been placed on difficulties which arise for those concerned with education as conceived of by the authors of this book. External and internal factors, which occasion this feeling of alienation, have been distinguished, and particular attention has been paid to the ways in which the authority structure and punishment system can intensify this predicament.

There are many who argue that the university and school can do little else but reflect the motivations and values of society; so nothing much, on this view, can be done about educational institutions unless the whole economic and social structure of society is radically altered. This is not a view that an educator need accept; for he can take the view that by encouraging critical thought, a teacher can be a source of challenge as well as of conservation. He can believe that if students can become committed to the purposes of an educational institution, and really become equipped as educated people to think and feel about social and personal problems, in time the values of educational institutions may have a widespread effect on society as a whole. This certainly happened after Arnold transformed the English Public Schools, whatever one thinks of the value system which they so effectively inculcated in their pupils; for after a lengthy period in such 'total institutions' a considerable body of able men went out who were actively committed to what the schools stood for and they put their principles into practice in a wide area of public life. They made a difference as a social movement.

If educational institutions are going to perform such a function on a wider scale under modern conditions, they will have to put their own houses in order. Their authority structure will have to be rationalized along lines which are in keeping with their purposes; their punishment systems will have to be humanized and put into proper perspective; and, above all, administrative and economic consideration must not lead to them being organized in such a depersonalized way that personal relationships with pupils become the prerogative of special counsellors. If their own internal arrangements were adapted better to forward their own purposes, at least they might be able to pursue their own purposes effectively.

They might even succeed in educating many of their students.

What the impact of such institutions on society as a whole would be is a matter for speculation. As was pointed out at the beginning, this chapter raises many questions which are properly the concern of the social scientist rather than of the philosopher. The point of philosophy is neither to prophesy nor necessarily to change the world. It is rather to get our predicament into a proper perspective, and to grasp better what reasons are good reasons for changing or for keeping things as they are. For not everything can or should be changed. Some things have to be endured; other things should be enjoyed.

In this book we have contented ourselves with exploring a perspective on central problems in education provided by the analysis of a widely current, specific concept of 'education'. We have attempted no justification of the values built into it; we have assessed no reasons for change or conservation. What we have tried to show, however, is that, *if* this view of education is assumed, the debates between progressives and traditionalists in education are largely anachronistic. There was little that was enjoyable in the traditional approach. Our hope is that we shall not have to endure for much longer the progressive protest against it.

Further Reading

This book is meant to be, in part, an introduction to some of the central problems in the philosophy of education. The point, therefore, of the following recommendations is to indicate where the student will be able to follow up in a more detailed and concentrated way topics which are raised in each chapter.

Chapter 1

The clearest and most readable treatment, at an elementary level, of the general problems of meaning and definition is to be found in Hospers, J., *An Introduction to Philosophical Analysis* (Routledge & Kegan Paul, 1967). Further points about definition, in the context of educational theory, can be found in Scheffler, I., *The Language of Education* (Charles Thomas, 1960) Ch. 1. The nature of philosophy of education is discussed at more length in the articles by Hirst, P. H., and Peters, R. S., in Tibble, J. (ed.), *The Study of Education* (Routledge & Kegan Paul, 1966) which is the parent volume of this series of monographs. References to other approaches to philosophy of education will also be found in these articles.

On the nature of concepts and on questions to do with their acquisition the student should consult Geach, P. T., *Mental Acts* (Routledge & Kegan Paul, 1957) Chs. 1-12, and Dearden, R. F., *The Philosophy of Primary Education* (Routledge & Kegan Paul, 1968) Ch. 6.

On more general issues concerning philosophy and conceptual analysis Hosper's introductory book should be supplemented by books presenting the historical development of modern philosophy such as Ryle, G. (*et al.*), *The Revolution in Philosophy* (Macmillan, 1956); Urmson, J. O., *Philosophical Analysis* (O.U.P., 1956); Passmore, J. A., *100 Years of Philosophy* (Duckworth, 1957); and Warncock, G. J., *English Philosophy since 1900* (O.U.P., 1958).

The collections of articles, Flew, A. G. N. (ed.), *Logic and Language* (Blackwell, 1951, 1953), provide good examples of modern conceptual analysis. The more recent Oxford readings in Philosophy also present, in paper-back form, many articles of relevance to the philosophy of education. Of particular relevance are Griffiths, A. P. (ed.), *Knowledge and Belief* (O.U.P., 1967); Parkinson, G. H. R. (ed.), *The Theory of Meaning* (O.U.P., 1968); Quinton, A. (ed.), *Political Philosophy* (O.U.P.,

1967); Foot, P. (ed.), *Theories of Ethics* (O.U.P., 1967); and White, A. (ed.), *The Philosophy of Action* (O.U.P., 1968).

The reference in Section 3 to Wittgenstein is to Wittgenstein, L., *Philosophical Investigations* (Blackwell, 1953) p. 32; and in Section 5 to Ryle is to Ryle, G., *The Concept of Mind* (Hutchinson, 1949).

These are both classics of modern philosophy and it would be impossible to refer the student to the spate of books and articles that have been written about them. Other classics, from rather different points of view, are Ayer, A. J., *Language, Truth, and Logic* (Faber, rev. ed. 1946); Popper, K. R., *Conjectures and Refutations* (Routledge & Kegan Paul, 1963); and Strawson, P. F., *Individuals* (Methuen, 1959).

Chapter 2

Questions raised in the introduction about the relevance to conduct of explanations in terms of unconscious motives, etc., can be followed up in Peters, R. S., *Authority, Responsibility and Education* (Allen & Unwin, 1959) Chs 4-6. The student may find that this little book of broadcast talks is a helpful way in to philosophical thinking generally; for its approach is via practical problems. More detailed treatment of the relevance of unconscious motives can be found in Peters, R. S., *The Concept of Motivation* (Routledge & Kegan Paul, 1958) Ch. 3; and MacIntyre, A., *The Unconscious* (Routledge & Kegan Paul, 1958).

Issues raised in Sections 1 and 2 on 'The concept of "education" ' and 'Aims of education' are more fully discussed in Peters, R. S., *Ethics and Education* (Allen & Unwin, 1966) Ch. 1, and in Dearden, R. F., Hirst, P. H., and Peters, R. S. (eds.), *Education and the Development of Reason* (Routledge & Kegan Paul, in preparation) which contains the paper by Peters entitled 'Education and the Educated Man' of which Section 1 is an abbreviation. This paper is also published in the *Proceedings of the Philosophy of Education Society of Great Britain*, 1970.

Section 3 on 'Contrasting approaches to content and method' opens up an extensive literature. The contrasts are further elaborated in articles by Peters, R. S., and Perry, L. R., in Archambault, R. D., *Philosophical Analysis and Education* (Routledge & Kegan Paul, 1965).

There is a critique of progressive education in Dearden, R. F., *The Philosophy of Primary Education* (Routledge & Kegan Paul, 1968) and in Peters, R. S. (ed.), *Perspectives on Plowden* (Routledge & Kegan Paul, 1969), and in Bantock, G. H., *Freedom and Authority in Education* (Faber, 1952).

Dewey, J., *Experience and Education* (Macmillan, 1938), should also be read in this context, together with the works of great educators such as Rousseau, Froebel, Montessori, and the Arnolds.

Price, Kingsley, *Education and Philosophic Thought* (Allyn & Bacon, 1962), attempts to present the thoughts of the more important figures in educational thought in an analytic way and L. R. Perry is the editor of a series published by Collier-Macmillan which deals with individual thinkers.

Arising from Section 4 on 'Needs and interests' a more detailed consideration of the concept of 'need' can be found in Maslow, A. H., *Motivation and Personality* (Harper, 1954); Peters, R. S., *The Concept of Motivation* (Routledge & Kegan Paul, 1958) Chs. 1 and 4; Benn, S. I., and Peters, R. S., *Social Principles and the Democratic State* (Allen & Unwin, 1959) Ch. 6; Komisar, B. P., ' "Need" and the Needs-Curriculum' in Smith, B. O., and Ennis, R. H., *Language and Concepts in Education* (Rand McNally, 1961).

The concept of 'interest' is examined in White, A. R., 'The Notion of Interest' in *Philosophical Quarterly*, Vol. 14, No. 57, 1964; Peters, R. S., *Ethics and Education* (Allen & Unwin, 1966) Ch. 6. The application of both concepts to education is dealt with in Dearden, R. F., *The Philosophy of Primary Education* (Routledge & Kegan Paul, 1968) Ch. 2. Classical uses of the concept of 'interest' can be studied in Dewey, J., *Interest and Effort in Education* (Houghton Mifflin, 1913); and Kilpatrick, W. H., *Philosophy of Education* (Macmillan, 1951) Ch. 20.

A survey of modern theories of 'intrinsic motivation' can be found in Hunt, J. McV., 'Intrinsic Motivation' in Levine, D. (ed.), *Nebraska Symposium on Motivation* (Univ. of Nebraska Press, 1965); and of the place of such theories in motivation theory generally in Peters, R. S., 'Motivation, Emotion, and the Conceptual Schemes of Common-sense' in Mischel, T. (ed.), *Human Action* (Academic Press, 1969).

Students who wish to go more thoroughly into psychological theories of motivation should tackle general text-books such as, Cofer, C. N., and Appley, M. H., *Motivation: Theory and Research* (Wiley, 1964) or Vernon, M. D., *Human Motivation* (C.U.P., 1969) in which the various theories are systematically set out.

Peters, R. S., *Ethics and Education* (Allen & Unwin, 1966), tackles explicitly the issues raised in Section 5 on 'The ethical basis of education', from a particular stand-point in ethical theory. It should be supplemented by a selection from general works on moral and political philosophy such as Brandt, R., *Ethical Theory* (Prentice Hall, 1959); Hospers, J., *Human Conduct* (Prentice Hall, 1961); Foot, P. (ed.), *Theories of Ethics* (O.U.P., 1967); Warnock, M., *Ethics since 1900* (O.U.P., 1960); MacIntyre, A., *A Short History of Ethics* (Routledge & Kegan Paul, 1967); Warnock, G. J., *Contemporary Moral Philosophy* (Macmillan, 1967); Quinton, A., *Political Philosophy* (O.U.P., 1967); Benn, S. I., and Peters, R. S., *Social Principles and the Democratic State* (Allen & Unwin, 1959); Barry, B., *Political Argument* (Routledge & Kegan Paul, 1965); and Laslett, P., and Runciman, W. G., *Philosophy, Politics, and Society* (Blackwell, 1957, 1962, and 1967. 1st, 2nd, and 3rd series).

Chapter 3

This chapter introduces in a simplified form most of the issues discussed in more detail in Dearden, R. F., Hirst, P. H., and Peters, R. S. (eds), *Education and the Development of Reason* (Routledge & Kegan Paul, in preparation).

On the concept of 'development' the student should consult Harris, D. B. (ed.), *The Concept of Development* (Univ. of Minnesota Press,

1957), in which the article by Nagel appears. Kohlberg's views are set out most clearly in Kohlberg, L. 'Early Education: A Cognitive Developmental View' in *Child Development*, Vol. 39, 1968; Kohlberg, L., 'Development of Moral Character and Ideology' in Hoffman, M. L. (ed.), *Review of Child Development Research*, Vol. 1 (Russell Sage, 1964); Kohlberg, L., 'Stage and Sequence: the Cognitive-Developmental Approach to Socialization', in Goslin, D. (ed.), *Handbook of Socialization* (Rand McNally, 1968); and in Turiel, E., 'Developmental Processes in the Child's Moral Thinking' in Mussen, P., Langer, J., and Covington, M., *Developmental Psychology* (Holt, Rinehart & Winston, 1969).

The background to Kohlberg's view can be found in Piaget, J., *The Moral Judgment of the Child* (Routledge & Kegan Paul, 1932). The most useful, if difficult, exposition of Piaget's theory is in Flavell, J., *The Developmental Theory of Jean Piaget* (Van Nostrand, 1963); and Furth, H., *Piaget and Knowledge* (Prentice Hall, 1969).

An exposition of his theory for teachers is in Furth, H., *Piaget for Teachers* (Prentice Hall, 1970).

On development theories generally students are advised to read Langer, J., *Theories of Development* (Holt, Rinehart, & Winston 1969). Of considerable historical importance, too, are the works of Arnold Gesell which should be consulted for background, together with standard works such as Baldwin, A. L., *Theories of Child Development* (John Wiley, 1967), and Maier, H. *Three Theories of Child Development* (Harper, 1965).

A philosophical critique of developmental theories can be found in Dearden, R. F., *The Philosophy of Primary Education* (Routledge & Kegan Paul, 1968); Peters, R. S. (ed.), *Perspectives on Plowden* (Routledge & Kegan Paul, 1969); and Hamlyn, D. W., 'The Logical and Psychological Aspects of Learning' in Peters, R. S. (ed.), *The Concept of Education* (Routledge & Kegan Paul, 1967).

A more advanced discussion of genetic psychology generally can be found in Mischel, T. (ed.), *Psychological and Epistemological Issues in the Development of Concepts* (Academic Press, 1970).

An examination of the place of 'mental health' in education is conducted in Peters, R. S., 'Mental Health as an Educational Aim' in Hollins, T. H. B. (ed.), *Aims in Education: A Philosophic Approach* (Manchester Univ. Press, 1964); and Wilson, J., *Education and the Concept of Mental Health* (Routledge & Kegan Paul, 1968).

References for further reading on the concept of 'person' can be found in the reading for Ch. 6.

Chapter 4

The general problems of curriculum planning are well set out in Taba, H., *Curriculum Development* (Harcourt, Brace and World, 1962). Some of the central issues are discussed from a more philosophical point of view in Broudy, H. S., Smith, B. O., and Burnett, J. R., *Democracy and Excellence in the American Secondary School* (Rand McNally, 1964).

A further discussion of the approach to different modes of knowledge and experience outlined here, is to be found in the paper by P. H. Hirst in Archambault, R. D. (ed.), *Philosophical Analysis and Education* (Routledge & Kegan Paul, 1965). There are a number of more substantial works which attempt mapping along similar lines; amongst these the reader may find the following of particular interest: Reid, L. A., *Ways of Knowledge and Experience* (Allen & Unwin, 1961); Oakeshott, M., *Experience and its Modes* (Cambridge University Press, 1966); Cassirer, E., *An Essay on Man* (Yale University Press, 1944), and Phenix, P. H., *Realms of Meaning* (McGraw Hill, 1964).

All such studies must be seen in relation to fundamental questions in epistemology both about the nature of knowledge in general and about the characteristic features of particular areas. I. Scheffler's two short books *Conditions of Knowledge* (Scott Foresman, 1965) and *Science and Subjectivity* (Bobbs-Merrill, 1967) form an excellent introduction to the general questions important in this context. For particular areas it is possible to list only a few works selected for their emphasis on the demarcatory features of various types of knowledge. Mitchell, B., *An Introduction to Logic* (Hutchinson, 1962); Korner, S., *The Philosophy of Mathematics* (Hutchinson, 1960); Nagel, E., *The Structure of Science* (Routledge & Kegan Paul, 1961); Harre, R., *An Introduction to the Logic of the Sciences* (Macmillan, 1960) are of immediate relevance. In connection with Chapter 3, work concerned with an understanding of persons has already been referred to, though questions about the nature of history and the social sciences have been a focus for much valuable discussion. *The Nature of Historical Explanation* (Oxford University Press, 1952) by Gardiner, P., and Winch, P., *The Idea of a Social Science* (Routledge & Kegan Paul, 1958) are of interest here, especially if read alongside the relevant chapters in Nagel's *The Structure of Science*. In the aesthetic domain there are two major introductory texts of note: Beardsley, M., *Aesthetics* (Harcourt, Brace and World, 1958) and Stolnitz, J., *Aesthetics and Philosophy of Art Criticism* (Houghton Mifflin, 1960). Ferre, F., *Basic Modern Philosophy of Religion* (Allen & Unwin, 1967) and Hepburn, R., *Christianity and Paradox* (Watts, 1958) focus the major problems of religious claims lucidly and forcefully. For works on ethics readers are referred to the suggestions for reading Ch. 2, and on the nature of philosophy, to the suggestions for Ch. 1.

Chapter 5

The concepts of 'teaching' and 'learning' are discussed in many introductory texts in philosophy of education, the relevant chapters in Langford, G., *Philosophy and Education* (Macmillan, 1968) being particularly worthy of comment. A group of influential papers on 'teaching' will be found in Macmillan, C. J. B., and Nelson, T. W. (eds.), *Concepts of Teaching* (Rand McNally, 1968). Papers on 'learning' and a number of more specific topics in this area, are to be found in two very useful collections: Komisar, B. P., and Macmillan, C. B. J. (eds), *Psychological Concepts in Education* (Rand McNally, 1967) and Smith, B. O., and

Ennis, R. H. (eds), *Language and Concepts in Education* (Rand McNally, 1961). Though at times philosophically more technical, Peters, R. S. (ed.), *The Concept of Education* (Routledge & Kegan Paul, 1967) contains a number of important contributions, not only on teaching and learning in general, but also on more specifically educational processes. The two papers by Dearden, R. F., on 'play', 'instruction' and 'learning by discovery' are of note here, as are chapters five and six of his book *The Philosophy of Primary Education* (Routledge & Kegan Paul, 1968). The collection by Peters, R. S., also contains a paper on 'indoctrination' by White, J. P., which takes further the discussion begun by Wilson, J., and Hare, R. M., in their contributions to Hollins, T. H. B. (ed.), *Aims in Education* (Manchester University Press, 1964).

Chapter 6

There has been little, if any, philosophical analysis done on the main conceptual issues discussed in this chapter. Philosophical background, however, can be sought on the concept of a 'person', though the student will find much of it very difficult. For instance the student can read the chapter on 'Persons' in Strawson, P. F., *Individuals* (Methuen, 1959), and that on 'The Concept of a Person' in Ayer, A. J., *The Concept of a Person and other Essays* (Macmillan, 1963), together with Hampshire, S., *Thought and Action* (Chatto & Windus, 1959).

There has also been some work done on 'Respect for Persons' following the treatment of this concept in Kant, I., *The Groundwork of the Metaphysic of Morals*. Recent examples are MacLagan, W. G., 'Respect for Persons as a Moral Principle' in *Philosophy*, July 1960; Peters, R. S., *Ethics and Education* (Allen & Unwin, 1966) Ch. 8; and Downey, R. S., and Telfer, E., *Respect for Persons* (Allen & Unwin, 1969).

There is, however, a dearth of philosophical analysis of the concept of 'personal relationships'. There is much reference to them in an ethico-religious context in MacMurray, J., *Reason and Emotion* (Fisher and Fisher, 1936); Buber, M., *Between Man and Man* (Fontana Press, 1961); and Eric Fromm deals with their importance, from a psychological stand-point, in Fromm, E., *The Art of Loving* (Harper, 1956).

There is, too, a brief treatment of their importance in teaching in Reid, L. A., *Philosophy and Education* (Heinemann, 1962) Ch. 10; and in Rogers, Carl R., *Freedom to Learn* (Charles Merrill, 1969). The chapters by Ben Morris on Freud and by A. V. Judges on Buber in Judges, A. V., *The Function of Teaching* (Faber & Faber, 1959), also deal with some of the issues with which this chapter is concerned.

Chapter 7

This chapter goes over again, in a greatly abbreviated form, much of the ground covered in the latter part of Peters, R. S., *Ethics and Education* (Allen & Unwin, 1966), which dealt with concepts such as 'freedom', 'authority', 'discipline' 'punishment', and 'democracy' in an educational context. It is, however, slanted rather differently towards modern controversies about alienation from and participation in educational institutions. The student will, no doubt, be familiar with much of the contemporary literature on these themes, though little of it is philosophical in its approach. An exception, however, is the University of Oxford *Report of the Committee on Relations with Junior Members* (O.U.P., 1969), which contains much reasoned argument from first principles. A historical background to the situation in America is provided by Jenks, C. and Riesman, D., *The Academic Revolution* (Doubleday, 1968), and fundamental issues about higher education are raised and discussed in Niblett, W. R. (ed.), *Higher Education: Demand and Response* (Tavistock Publications, 1969).

Index of proper names

Subject index

Accommodation, 45
achievements, 38, 61, 62, 65, 75, 83, 85, 91, 92
activities, 91, 94-5, 106
  of learning, 84, 86
  of teaching, 84, 86, 89-90
  worth-while, 103-4, 123
administrators, 106, 108, 111, 115, 117, 120
aesthetic, 13, 27, 39, 50, 54, 58, 62, 64, 69, 71, 92, 110
affect (see feeling)
aims,
  concept of, 26-7
  of education, 19, 25-8, 31, 32, 33-6, 40, 57, 60, 103, 119, 127
alienation, 108, 111-12, 121, 124, 129, 130
arithmetic, 29, 69, 70, 128
art, 12, 92
assimilation, 45
attitudes, 78, 93, 96, 97, 109, 110-11, 120, 126
authoritarian, approach to education, 14, 28-32, 42, 48, 104
authoritarianism, 111, 112, 120, 123
authority, 7, 11, 12, 46
  an, 114, 115-16, 124
  concept of, 41, 113-14
  figures of, 112, 123, 128
  provisional, 117, 122, 124
  rationalization of, 114-24, 130
  structure of, 106, 107, 108, 111-12, 113, 116-22, 130
  of teacher, 14, 101
autonomy, 27, 31, 32, 34, 35, 40, 53, 54, 57, 58, 61, 125, 126

academic, 116-22
functional, 38
of headmaster, 121

Belief, 13, 44, 50, 63, 78
  grounds of, 22
benevolence, 36, 90, 96, 102, 115
biology, influence of, 30-2, 42, 43, 44, 52, 58

Categories, 9, 64-6
causality, 9, 44, 47, 55, 64, 81
central cases, 12
chemistry, 10
child-centred, approach to education, 14, 28-32, 33-9, 42, 48, 52, 88, 104, 124
children,
  interests of, 30, 31, 32-9
  less able, 83
  needs of, 31, 32-9
choice, 11, 29, 32, 45, 53, 67, 91-2, 97, 117, 126
coercion, 12, 30, 33, 46, 124, 125, 127, 129
cognition, 60, 85
  importance of, 39, 49-50, 62
cognitive,
  stage theory, 46-53
  state of learner, 80-2
  stimulation, 47, 48
  structure, 47
colleges of education, 42
commands, 7, 123
communication, 111, 121
community, educational, 14, 15